THE DECADE OF REALIGNMENT

The Leadership Speeches of David Steel (1976-1986)

by
Stuart Mole

ACKNOWLEDGEMENTS

Our thanks for permission to use copyright photographs and cartoons as follows:—

cover photo	Neil Libbert (The Observer)
cover design	Oliver Dick
foreword photo	Ronn Ballantyne
Chapter 1	The Guardian
Chapter 2	Gibbard, The Guardian 23/3/77
Chapter 3	Garland, Daily Telegraph 15/12/77
Chapter 4	The Guardian
Chapter 5	The Scotsman
Chapter 6	The Guardian
Chapter 7	Liberal News
Chapter 8	Financial Times
Chapter 9	Bill Caldwell, The Star 8/7/83
Conclusion	Garland, Daily Telegraph 15/12/77

Published by Hebden Royd Publications Ltd, The Birchcliffe Centre, Hebden Bridge, West Yorkshire HX7 8DG.

Typeset by Banbury Typesetters Ltd, Borough House, Marlborough Road, Banbury, Oxon OX16 8TH

Printed by T. Snape and Co Ltd, Boltons Court, Preston, Lancashire.

ISBN 1 85187 038 5

Contents

David Steel and family at Ettrick Bridge.

Foreword

To be required to read one's own speeches over the past ten years is an eerie experience. Would they be full of tedious repetition from year to year, or worse, internal contradictions? After all, I never look back on the previous year's Assembly speech when starting to draft the next one. I must therefore admit to having been pleasantly surprised that there did seem after all to have been a coherence and continuity through the decade.

But a book of speeches on their own could be just dull, self-indulgent or a stroll through past memories. With his perceptive commentary on each year's events Stuart Mole has successfully placed each utterance in context and reminded us of the state of the political map in each year of the decade.

I should explain how these speeches are put together. Throughout the year I tuck away items of interest in a file which I take home to Ettrick Bridge over the summer recess. Early in September I start to write the outline of what I want to say and invite a small group of "advisers" (a word I hate) to contribute thoughts on one or two particular points — Nadir Dinshaw on race, William Wallace on international tensions — and so on. John Pardoe when he was in the Commons would suggest lines on the economy. Not all of these contributions were always used, nor their originators always pleased with the end result. Other friends and colleagues, Norman Hackett, David Alton, and others have added ideas.

Richard Holme, who has been in on every one of these preparations, usually joins me for a couple of days in Ettrick Bridge, where he walks my black labrador over the hill at ungodly hours of the morning and returns with fresh inspiration. My sitting room floor is littered with cuttings and my indecipherable pages of handwriting, for that is how I prefer to work. Judy supplies endless mugs of tea and coffee and large helpings of constructive criticism.

A first draft is dispatched to one of my long suffering secretaries and the aim is to arrive at the Assembly with a full first draft. The hectic nature of the Assembly week with all its engagements, press and broadcasting interviews plus as much listening to debates from the platform as possible does not allow for much speech writing. (I moved the leader's speech from Saturday morning to Friday afternoon mainly because I hate morning speeches but that gives even less time to prepare).

Throughout the Assembly, the speech is continually dismembered and discussed in the light of what is going on at the conference. There are re-drafting sessions, late into the night long after most delegates have gone or should have gone to bed, involving the advisers and my full time political assistant of the day, Archy Kirkwood, Andrew Gifford, Stuart Mole and Graham Watson.

The text has to be retyped several times with a press edition prepared through the final night. It is always too long. We haggle over what to "lose", or whether some witticism might be misunderstood. The most famous dispute occurred over the coalition section of the very first speech when some present implored me to omit it, and I hesitated for a while before leaving it in.

An added horror of recent years has been the advent of the autocue machine which supposedly projects the text on to glass screens. President Reagan regularly uses it. So does Mrs Thatcher. I have found it more trouble than it is worth. The "toilet roll" text is difficult to prepare, and there was one moment of pure farce last year when I tugged at one length which appeared to be stuck under a chair only to discover Stuart in the far corner of the hotel suite angrily pulling at the other. The television lights usually blind the screens anyhow. So then it's back to the typewritten page.

I question whether this is the right method of political oratory. I certainly never wrote and read a speech before I became Party Leader. But the demands of press deadlines and TV directors require an advance text. The utterances of the party leaders are minutely dissected by the commentators, so each phrase has to be properly weighed. Mr Gladstone and Mr Lloyd George had not these problems and their speeches were no doubt all the better for that.

I leave Stuart Mole to comment on the events of the decade. I simply wish to record my thanks to him and to the others who have so untiringly helped this compilation over the years.

David Steel
July 1986

In 1986, David Steel celebrates his tenth anniversary as Leader of the Liberal Party.

David Steel was born in Scotland in 1938 and was educated in Nairobi, Kenya, and in Edinburgh. He graduated from Edinburgh University with an M.A. in 1960 and an LL.B. in 1962. He was President of the University Liberal Club and of the Students' Representative Council.

He was Assistant Secretary to the Scottish Liberal Party from 1962-1964, and became the youngest member of the 1964-1966 Parliament when he was elected MP for Roxburgh, Selkirk and Peebles in the by-election of 1965. He was President of the Anti-Apartheid Movement from 1967-1970, and he reformed the law on abortion with his Private Member's Bill of 1967.

He has travelled widely throughout the world, is a frequent lecturer in the United States and a regular visitor to African nations.

David Steel was the Liberal Chief Whip from 1970-75, and was elected Leader of the Liberal Party in 1976. He became the youngest Privy Counsellor in 1977. A former TV reporter for BBC Scotland, he is a regular contributor to *The Times*, *The Guardian* and other journals, and the author of a number of pamphlets, the most recent being *Sharing Profits* (1986). He has also written *No Entry: The Background and Implications of the Commonwealth Immigrants Act 1968, David Steel's Border Country, A House Divided*, and edited *Partners in One Nation*.

Acknowledgements

My special thanks go to Charlene Lee-Ling, Graham Watson, Michael Duncan and Katherine Little for their help in producing this book. I am also grateful for the speed and efficiency with which Tony Greaves and all at Hebden Royd met the very tight publishing deadline.

I must take sole responsibility for the opinions and accuracy of all that I have written. While David Steel has read the text, he has made no attempt to interfere with my interpretation of events, which remain my own. Having from time to time suggested to him that he publish his collected Assembly speeches as Leader, I am glad that he has chosen to cajole me into undertaking the task, with publication timed to coincide with the celebrations of a fitting tenth anniversary — his election as Liberal Leader.

Stuart Mole
June 1986

Stuart Mole voted for John Pardoe in the 1976 Liberal leadership election. That notwithstanding, from 1975 he served as Press Officer to David Steel and the Liberal MPs and, after the 1979 Election, became Head of David Steel's Private Office and his Personal Assistant. A Borough Councillor since 1972 and four times Liberal Parliamentary candidate for Chelmsford, Stuart Mole currently works at the Commonwealth Secretariat where he is the Assistant Director in the Commonwealth Secretary-General's Private Office.

1976

Declaration of the leadership election.

Chapter One

A new political agenda

On the night of 7 July, in Poplar Civic Hall, David Steel became the first Leader of the Liberal Party to be elected by the membership as a whole, as opposed to his Parliamentary colleagues. Almost 70,000 party members had voted, and the two candidates, Steel and Pardoe, had criss-crossed the country, speaking to packed and enthusiastic meetings. There were few policy differences between them, with both regarded as being on the 'radical' wing of the Party. Of the two, Steel's radicalism credentials were impressive: President of the Anti-Apartheid Movement, architect of the Abortion Act 1967 and noted campaigner for human rights. Pardoe's was a more mercurial radicalism, occasionally bursting the banks of prudence and sometimes having as strong appeal to the Right as to the Left.

But where differences arose it was about style and strategy. Pardoe seemed to be the clear favourite of the party activists. They liked his aggressive and abrasive style, his intellectual dynamism and his clear analysis of the Party's future. If Pardoe appealed to the heart, excited by his rumbustious claim to be 'an effective bastard', Steel's appeal was to the head: his solid record, his clear ability as a publicist, his shrewd toughness, his calm pragmatism and his obvious electoral appeal, through television in particular, to a wider electorate.

It was Steel who managed to goad Pardoe to go 'over the top' — with a crafty piece of provocation — and who thereby demonstrated his own dependability under pressure. Life with Pardoe might be more fun, thought many, but perhaps a little too dangerous. Steel seemed the safe bet; even if they were later to learn that the dramatic course he was to chart was nothing of the kind.

By the end of the campaign, the result was not in doubt although the margin of victory was impressive. Steel polled 12,541 'national' votes (weighted by constituency, after membership ballots) to Pardoe's 7,032. It was a result which was as popular among the party rank-and-file as it was in the country as a whole.

That much was satisfying enough. But if Steel's own life had taken a new course, it would only be worth it, in the end, if the Liberal Party itself was to prosper.

Steel had a number of important preoccupations that August, as his mind turned to his first major test — the Liberal Assembly in Llandudno.

First, he had to capitalise on his decisive victory in the election by pulling the Party together, restoring its shaken morale and giving it a new direction. There were difficulties. John Pardoe, it is true, had gracefully conceded defeat and appealed for all in the Party to give Steel their loyalty and enthusiasm; but he had clearly been affected by his defeat and upset at some of the tactics which had helped bring that about. Yet he was an indispensable member of any Parliamentary team and had to be brought on board.

More immediately, Cyril Smith, who had campaigned wholeheartedly for Pardoe, took the result badly and threatened not to visit any of the constituencies which had voted for Steel. Happily, it was not a boycott he maintained for long.

Although, on balance, the leadership election campaign had been good for the Party, generating national publicity and raising the spirits of the membership, the shock of the Thorpe affair and his subsequent resignation had severely damaged morale and enthusiasm.

The second difficult task facing the new Leader was therefore related to the first and was to rally the Party by giving it new purpose.

A different leader — and probably most leaders — would have chosen the Assembly to pacify and reassure, to exhort and inspire — and not to throw the Party into controversy or alarm. The difficult questions would have been set aside for another time. Reconciliation would have been the sole intent.

But that was not to be Steel's way. From the first moments of his Parliamentary career, Steel had exhibited what for some Liberals was a distressing character defect — he was interested in power: in the Party sinking its teeth into what Jo Grimond had called 'the red meat of politics', and undoubtedly in wielding power himself.

The clear method by which this could be achieved was through a political realignment which could give the Liberal Party a pivotal role.

The idea was not new. Jo Grimond had argued the case for a non-socialist radical alternative and came close to putting his early ideas of co-operation to the test when Harold Wilson's wafer-thin majority of 1964 looked like disappearing altogether a year later. The moment passed, and the notion slipped from fashion — but not from the mind of David Steel, and for reasons that were as practical as they were intellectual.

Steel has never been attracted by millennial liberalism — by using his position as an MP as a Liberal mystic, wandering the country and reassuring the faithful few that their belief was sure and that one day they would indeed inherit the kingdom. As an active MP from a tiny Parliamentary Party, he saw clearly that he could only achieve anything at all by co-operation — by non-party campaigning and by working across the political divide. Further, he recognised that, even with the Liberal objective of power in its own right, the electoral arithmetic made it almost inevitable that in breaking the two-party system, multi-party politics would become the norm, at least for a while. That meant co-operation would be a necessity — more especially so if the introduction of proportional representation was to stabilise and reflect that new reality.

Realignment surfaced once again — without a great deal of success — with the launch in 1968 of the Radical Action Movement. Later, after the debacle of the 1970 election which saw a traumatic fall in the number of Liberal MPs from twelve to six, Steel toyed with the none-too-popular idea of a limited electoral pact with Labour. But, above all, it was the result of the 1974 election — with its large Liberal vote of six million, the offer of a place in Government from Ted Heath, its minority Labour administration and its hung Parliament — which brought a frightened Liberal Party face to face with the coalition issue.

It was not an argument that Jeremy Thorpe, or many in the Party, were prepared to follow through, but for Steel it became central to his thinking and at the heart of his campaign for the leadership.

He spent the summer handwriting and re-writing his speech at his home in Ettrick Bridge, and this was to be his message at Llandudno, despite warnings of trouble from a jittery Party and suspicious Young Liberals. Indeed, a demonstration on the floor of the Assembly was threatened if the word 'coalition' should pass his lips.

Nonetheless, Steel rejected private pleas to tone down the text.

Unless the issue could be confronted now, he reasoned, it might rumble on for years. In any case, he had a special authority as the first directly-elected Leader of the Party. He chose to exercise that authority at once, when it was at its most fresh. It was a point he made at the outset:

> This has been an extraordinary year for Liberals. We have had three leaders during it, which is some going, even by the standards of Liberal history.
>
> But the particular responsibility of the leader is substantial, and I want to begin by reminding you that I inherit a much stronger Liberal position than did either of my immediate predecessors. That this is so is due in large measure to their personal qualities. Jo Grimond took over an ageing and divided Party with the popular support of only 2.7% of the electorate. By his magnetism he attracted into it a younger generation and launched it afresh with new ideas. This Party will always owe him an incalculable debt of gratitude, not only for his ten years of restorative leadership, but for his services this year, when he again took over the reins to see us through a complex period of internal constitutional and political change.
>
> Jeremy Thorpe, in taking over after Jo Grimond, expanded the popular vote of the Liberal Party in an unprecedented way. There can be few politicians of modern times who are as capable as he has been in triumphing over adversity and of galvanising his supporters by that almost unique boundless energy. The enthusiasm and drive which he brought to the Party in his years as leader will not be forgotten by us.
>
> Now I have two advantages over my immediate predecessors. The first is that I have been elected by the mass membership of the Party, and not, as they were, by that loosely-knit group of politically motivated men called the Parliamentary Liberal Party. I hope that this will help to end the disturbing trend towards talk of 'the Party' on the one hand and 'the Parliamentary Party' on the other. We are one movement, and you have given me the authority to lead it.
>
> I am not expected in this role to be the Party's organiser nor its fund-raiser, but to lead it — which with the help of my team of colleagues in Parliament and other elected organs of the Party I intend to do.
>
> The second advantage is that there is now clearly established machinery for getting rid of me. All you need is seven MPs or fifty constituency associations. In all seriousness, I hope that these facts will help create a closer bond between the leader and the party in the country.
>
> In my speech on being elected leader, I declared that there was a generation's work of reform ahead of us. I say that again deliberately. The only trouble is, we haven't got that length of time to do it.

He went on to underline his belief that the political system had stagnated and that neither Conservative nor Labour Governments could act in the long term interest of the nation as a whole.

There is nothing that can be altered by another simple change or swapping of the two front benches.

When the Tory or Labour politicians talk of a return to normality, they are thinking of reducing the dole queue, or notching up the value of the pound a few points, or returning us to the conditions of 1959 or 1968 or 1971, or some halcyon days of their choice.

That won't do for Liberals. We face the fact that the country requires radical changes in the way we have conducted ourselves since the war. We have to work to change popular values and expectations, and to reverse the whole thrust of Government policies, trade union demands and business beliefs.

To put things right we must start by taking a long-term view.

The Parties we have had in government have been devoted only to their own interests, and at most to the pragmatic management of the country's affairs. They have abandoned national leadership, and failed to set out long-term aims and objects to inject a sense of purpose into our lives.

When I say that the nation should talk about the long-term, I am not thinking of marginally increased productivity, or some lowering of taxation, or just winning the next election for the Party of our choice. I am talking about creating the kind of society of which we would be proud members, instead of the present one, of which many feel ashamed.

We can make a start by declaring the fundamental opposition of Liberals to the steady drift towards the creation of a corporate state, which has taken place under Conservative and Labour Governments.

The sovereignty and freedom of the people depends for enduring security upon the supremacy of a freely elected Parliament, and no sectional interest should be pressed to the detriment of that supremacy.

Yet the impression is gaining ground that the only citizens who have power to influence and control events are members of the Cabinet, directors of the C.B.I., and leaders of the major trades unions. It is a trend which we as a Liberal Party are determined to fight.

You will look in vain for policies to revive the authority of Parliament in the Tory and Labour manifestos.

The answer lay in proportional representation to boost the authority of parliament and in longer-term economic policies to 'elevate the merits of frugality and thrift in the conduct of our affairs' and to make a concerted attack on the rising levels of poverty. It required tax reform and the introduction of profit sharing as an incentive to the workforce.

But even if we achieve all these economic objectives we shall not have ushered in the millenium. Economic recovery will not be enough. A growth in real material prosperity and its more equitable sharing will not of themselves bring about the changes necessary to create a Liberal society.

We have after all raised standards of living under Labour and Conservative Governments. But they have utterly failed to raise the opportunities for individual fulfilment and enhance value in life. Quite the reverse, they have let such opportunities shrink. Liberals are dedicated to expanding them.

Look at the quality of life today. Thousands of children are taught in schools which in the name of progress are far too large to enable the pupils to be anything more than statistics instead of a developing human personality.

Millions of our people live in homes which are on large housing estates of the kind graphically described by Billy Connolly as 'a desert with windows'.

Countless men and women go to toil daily in oversized industries where the management and ownership cannot help but be remote, and where they are treated not as human beings with ideas to contribute but as mere units of production.

In many ways we are ahead of schedule on 1984. The slogan 'small is beautiful' must become an integral part of the Liberal message and approach to every aspect of policy.

The problem lay in the stifling of individual initiative by the centralised state apparatus. Nursery schools, playgrounds and small rural bus services were all desperately needed, but legislation prevented citizens getting together under their own initiative to provide these services.

All that I am saying adds up to a plea for less Government control, regulation and restraint. Why should we always look to Government to solve problems when we can solve them ourselves? The 'nanny' attitude to government has been encouraged by Tory and Labour administrations. We must change all this. Let us put back the frontiers of government.

Government should simply make it possible for others to take initiatives, not clasp everything to its own bosom. I want to create a decent humility about what governments can achieve. They cannot, as some politicians believe, legislate for Utopia. Government is not the only source of positive social action, but the people of this country have been conditioned to look to 'them' instead of being encouraged to operate together in their own communities. I was in Belfast last week. The only ray of hope there has come not from any government but from the housewives who have founded the Peace Movement. The scope for action by communities themselves is enormous.

I believe that what is required from government is less legislation and more imagination. The torrents of legislation reflect not only the regular reversal of other sides' policies, but the bureaucratic and predictable nature of their output has a lot to do with a highly competent and able but over large civil service with too great a respect for precedent, and its eye always on hierarchy.

We must as Liberals lead the fightback against collectivism and statism. Look at the way the other Parties in government have treated the small businessman, the self-employed, or attempts to form co-operatives — as infernal nuisances in an otherwise ordered society.

The Tories claim to champion 'liberty', though a very different kind from ourselves. The Labour Party has cornered 'equality' though of a very different kind from ourselves. But we alone bang the drum of fraternity.

It was not until almost the end that he began to build his argument for a new strategy, and to deliver his challenge to Liberals to take 'the bumpy road'.

The nation is weary of the failure of old policies and spent men. We have to proclaim that it is possible to break out of the stagnant political order and the straitjacket of the two-party system.

A new society is struggling to be born in this tired country. We must help it slough off the old skin. We are on the side of the future and we are the only agent of hope and of change.

But if we are to succeed as a Party we need certain changes of attitude among others and amongst ourselves. There is no place for the Liberal Party in the soft cosy centre of political debate. We must be away out forward. We must capture the new ground and the high ground of politics.

There are two groups of people to whom I want particularly to appeal. The first is the small 'l' liberals who have up to now believed that the right course is to work within one of the two bigger Parties. Theirs is no longer a tenable position. Their influence on the Tory and Labour Parties has been minimal. The Tories lurch rightward, and the Labour Party drifts on as an uneasy coalition between illiberal state Socialists who make all the running and Social Democrats who get dragged along behind.

It is no secret that I count many members of other parties among my friends, that I value their company and discussion with them. But I have long since abandoned hope that their private views may be translated into public action. Even those who occasionally translate private views into public talk are to be found tamely in the lobby when the whip cracks.

The fact that they must face is that if liberal values are to be preserved and developed it can only be through the regeneration of the Liberal Party. Those who have preened themselves as repositories of wisdom and light in the other parties have sold out to the system. [Their impotence is nowhere more perfectly symbolised than in the irrelevant gesture of the

Foreign Secretary's black tie at a white tie banquet in New York.]

The second group to whom we must appeal is that generation which has stood aside, not from particular causes, but from the follow through of political commitment. Now is not the time to be standing on the sidelines complaining that the game is too dirty. Only for so long can you remain blinkered in dedication to a particularly worthy cause without seeing the need for large-scale fundamental change which can only come about through total political action. We want those who have until now been repelled by the party political process, by its false promises, by its narrowness of vision, by its short-term expedients, to come in now and help us build a new nation.

I also said we need to alter attitudes ourselves. I have three things in mind.

First, we've got to be ready and enthusiastic to welcome others into our ranks. I am appalled sometimes by the attitudes of deep suspicion which greets newcomers, particularly if they are nationally known. We must stop behaving like one of the purer sects of the exclusive brethren.

I remember as a very new candidate in my constituency hearing the good news that after I had talked with a woman of previously mild Tory allegiance, who was in our own jargon an 'opinion leader' in one of the towns, she had decided to support me. When the local branch met to elect a new committee I suggested her name. My stalwart Liberals frowned. 'Oh we don't want her', said one, 'she's a turncoat'. 'Yes', I said, 'and if we're going to win this seat from the Tories we need to find another 4,765 turncoats.' And we did, and more.

Next, we really must improve our own internal organisation and communication. At the last Party Council meeting, when I spoke of the tortuous nature of our constitution and our procedures and the difficulty of getting quick decisions on anything, I was accused by one of our most formidable candidates of seeking to introduce into our Party 'creeping efficiency'. I plead guilty. I don't even ask for galloping efficiency. Creeping efficiency will do.

Third, and most important, we must follow through the logical consequences of our own policies and utterances if we are to convince the public that we really mean business when we talk about being the only agent of hope and change.

Let there be no misunderstanding. We are in being as a political party to form a government so as to introduce the policies for which we stand. That is our clear aim and object. But I as leader have a clear obvious duty to assess how most speedily we can reach that objective. I do not expect to lead just a nice debating society.

If we argue that we alone can be the means of transforming the sterility of British political life; if we tell the public that only by voting Liberal in sufficient numbers to prevent one other Party gaining a majority, will we achieve electoral reform, and break the Tory/Labour stranglehold, then equally we must be clear in our own minds that if the political conditions are right (which of course they were not in February, 1974), and if our own values are retained, we shall probably have — at least temporarily — to share power with somebody else to bring about the changes we seek.

(Interruption!)

Of course neither of the other Parties will want to relinquish their exclusive alternating hold on power, but if the people won't let them have it then they will both have to lump it — Tory and Labour.

I want the Liberal Party to be the fulcrum and centre of the next election argument — not something peripheral to it. If that is to happen we must not give the impression of being afraid to soil our hands with the responsibilities of sharing power.

We must be bold enough to deploy the coalition case positively. We must go all out to attack the other parties for wanting power exclusively to themselves no matter how small a percentage of public support.

If people want a more broadly-based government they must vote Liberal to get it. And if they vote Liberal we must be ready to help provide it.

What I am saying is that I want the Liberals to be an altogether tougher and more determined force. I want us to be a crusading and campaigning movement, not an academic think-tank nor minority influence nor occasional safety-valve in the political system.

The road I intend to travel may be a bumpy one, and I recognise therefore the risk that in the course of it we may lose some of the passengers, but I don't mind so long as we arrive at the end of it reasonably intact and ready to achieve our goals.

None of us in this party is interested in office for office's sake. If we were we would never have joined the Liberal Party. But we are fighting to achieve those things in which we believe, for which this party stands, and we must be prepared to do that in the most effective way possible.

There are some issues on which there can never under any circumstances be the slightest compromise. We cannot, for example, ever do anything which would take away from our absolute commitment to fight the obscenity of racialism, whether at home or abroad. I am tired of the well-meaning politicians who go around apologising for the variety of communities in these islands, as though this was not always part of our evolving nation.

Freedom is indivisible. If one man or one nation lacks it, we ourselves are less free. There will be some who say — in the Liberal Party as well as outside it — that Britain alone must come first, and if others starve or suffer from repression that is their problem, and none of our concern. That is not and never can be a Liberal attitude.

This has been for Liberals an anxious year, a rough year, at times a miserable year.

Many people looking in on this conference must have been wondering: why do these Liberals go on? They throw themselves into battle only to suffer defeat after defeat, with the occasional false dawn.

This year many of you may have wondered whether you should give it all up. You could have had more time with your families, dug your garden, or still with a sense of social responsibility devoted your time to any one of a number of good causes. And if you have felt so tempted, there is no need to feel ashamed. For so have I, and so at one time or another have most of us on this platform.

But we are here because we are heirs to a great tradition. We have been meeting this week here in Llandudno, in Lloyd George's old constituency. Had it not been for those who have more recently gone before us to preserve and maintain the Liberal Party when many doubted the need, then the condition of the country today would demand that men and women come together to conspire to invent it.

Progress in politics is in a strange way like mountaineering. You rope a team together, you prepare a base camp and higher camps, only to be beaten back again and again by adverse circumstances, or falter in your advance because some have lost their foothold and we all slip back a little.

You have chosen me to be the lead man; not the entire expedition, but the one who searches for the fingerholds and determines the precise route which we should take.

It's time to start the next assault. The clouds are moving away and the summit is coming again into view.

Together we can reach that summit.

A few months ago I stood at the grave of Robert Kennedy on the hillside of Arlington Cemetery in Washington. There on the stark white wall are carved a few sentences of that memorable speech he delivered just ten years ago in South Africa.

"Each time a man stands for an ideal, or acts to improve the lot of others, or strikes out against injustice, he sends forth a tiny ripple of hope."

What I ask you to do now is to go out from this great Assembly, back to your constituencies to send out ripples of hope — that they swell and join together to form across our land an irresistible floodtide of reform.

The word had been uttered. A noisy demonstration, drowned by the cheers of the majority, had marked the release of the taboo subject from the closet. But few expected then that the jump from theory to practice would be quite so precipitous.

1977

'Oh, I'll quite understand if you don't catch me — but are you sure you want me to go through the bottom of your boat?'

Chapter Two

Militant for the reasonable man

The controversy raised by the Llandudno speech continued to smoulder through the winter of 1976, with the debate fanned into fresh life by David Steel, who returned to the subject in a party political broadcast in November. But by early 1977, it was becoming evident that the Government's tenuous hold over the House of Commons was weakening fast. The loss of Walsall North and Workington to the Conservatives had removed the Government's overall majority, but it had been sustained in practice by the votes of eleven Scottish Nationalists and three Plaid Cymru MPs. The Nationalists saw the Devolution Bill for Scotland and Wales then before Parliament as their major priority.

The effective emasculation of the Bill, by the loss of a timetable motion which would have prevented the Bill being 'talked out', outraged the Nationalists. Their sole reason for keeping the Government in power disappeared and they had every hope that an early General Election, which could be fought around the Home Rule issue in Scotland and Wales, might be to their electoral advantage.

The crunch came in March 1978, with the defeat in Parliament of part of the austerity package of public spending cuts imposed by the International Monetary Fund as the price for helping Britain through her severe economic problems. From that moment, until the No Confidence Debate six days laters (on a motion tabled by Margaret Thatcher, the Leader of the Opposition) the idea of the Lib/Lab Pact began to take root. As far as Steel was concerned, the initiative for an agreement had to be taken by the Government. Despite the predictions of the press that frightened Liberal MPs were likely to abstain, rather than precipitate an unwelcome General Election, the Liberal Leader publicly announced two possible courses of action, neither involving abstention. Either the Government could negotiate Liberal support for an agreed package of measures, in the national interest, for the next two years; or else the Liberals would vote for a General Election. The one thing they were not prepared to do was to stagger on, from vote to vote, with a 'lame-duck Labour programme'. And to underline the deadly seriousness of his intent, Steel ordered the Party Organisation on to a war-footing for a likely General Election.

After a flurry of activity over the weekend, the Government got the message and began to explore the real possibility of an agreement with the Liberals. The Government's caution and hesitation was more than matched by nervousness among the ranks of the Parliamentary Liberal Party. After a series of feverish meetings over the Monday and Tuesday, the deal was done. The Liberals would agree to support the Labour Government in the division lobbies at the conclusion of Wednesday's No Confidence debate. In return, the Cabinet endorsed the basis for the Lib/Lab Agreement, the principal elements of which were: a joint Consultative Committee to review Government business; a system of regular contact between Government Ministers and their Liberal counterparts; and the Government's acceptance of a number of key policy objectives, including the reintroduction of the Devolution Bill for Scotland and Wales and the pledge to bring in a Bill for Direct Elections to the European Parliament. The Government was saved; and the Conservative opposition thrown into the dangerous anger of those who had scented blood but seen their quarry flee to safety at the final moment.

By the time the Liberal Leader came to address the Liberal Assembly at Brighton that September the Pact had been in being for barely six months. It was a time for explanation, reassurance and a steady nerve. The electoral omens were not good. The County Council elections in May had been disastrous and the experience of Parliamentary by-elections was that two party cooperation was a difficult concept to sell to a sceptical electorate — especially in the face of an overwhelmingly hostile and pro-Tory press. Furthermore, there had already been one or two notable hiccups, most notably over the

Government's 5p levy on petrol tax which the Liberals had vigorously opposed.

It was evident that the Brighton conference would be dominated by the Pact and would need careful handling from the start. Steel therefore chose to make two speeches — both at the opening and at the end of the Assembly. It was a tiring exercise and not one he has ever chosen to repeat. But his opening speech was designed to set the tone for the week. Inevitably, it was therefore confined to a single topic:

> It has been a somewhat unusual and tumultuous year. As one Liberal wrote to me: "We understood from your speech last year that you were keen on marriage but we didn't expect to find ourselves pushed to the altar quite so soon". To be candid neither did I! But I take the point, and it is only right that at the outset of our annual assembly I explain what we have been doing and why. Reluctant though I have been to divide what I have to say into two parts I want to concentrate this afternoon on the current political situation and our role in it, and return on Saturday to the longer-term development of Liberalism.
>
> I freely admit that I did underestimate some of the problems in the agreement between ourselves and the Government. I underestimated the difficulty of putting over what we were trying to do; I underestimated the rage of the Tories and their allies in the Press, thwarted of what they still think of as their rightful inheritance. Incidentally let us note the double standards — the Conservative Government elected in 1959 went on to within weeks of its 5 year maximum term of office despite great mid-term unpopularity and loss of seats at by-elections. I underestimated how much the British people have been taught to think of politics as "picking sides". I underestimated how frightened we have become in this country of innovation, of trying to do things a better way.
>
> But I have never for one minute underestimated the significance of the step my colleagues and I decided to take last March. It was a decision of great constitutional importance and, however much it may be misrepresented by those who prefer the drama of confrontation politics, it marked the beginning of the return to sanity in this divided country. Negotiation, with patient bargaining and compromise, may not call for high adrenalin and screaming headlines but it does call for something more important: patience, persistence and judgement.
>
> Our critics are not sure whether we have gained too much or too little: I am alternatively portrayed as the youthful dupe of wily old men, or the Frankenstein monster which has risen to terrorise his erstwhile master. Mr Ian Mikardo declared that Mr Callaghan has handed over the choice of date of the next election to me. If that's so, I must confess to you, the Prime Minister forgot to tell me.

Well history will have to judge where the balance of party advantage lies. I care much more for the long overdue emergence of the national interest as the proper standard of political decision.

It has long been our view as Liberals that there should be fixed parliamentary terms subject only to the government retaining the confidence of parliament. We have opposed the uncertainty and unfairness which a Prime Minister's arbitrary right of dissolution inflicts on the country. We have also in recent years campaigned against too frequent changes of policy direction by government which have prevented coherent long-term economic planning.

It was against the background of these two attitudes that we met as a parliamentary party in March to consider the motion of no confidence tabled by the leader of the opposition. We knew that our votes could be decisive in bringing about a third general election in three years, something which scarcely anybody outside the ranks of the Conservative Party, and only some inside, thought to be in the national interest.

There was one preliminary matter we had to settle among ourselves. I knew how damaging in the history of the Liberal Party had been splits when Liberal MPs regularly voted in opposite lobbies on major issues. These occurred in the pre-war parliament and indeed post-war as Frank Byers, who was chief whip after the war, will tell you. It took years — until after the 1964 election in fact — to get over that image in the public mind. I therefore told my colleagues that although following my talk with the Prime Minister I was going to argue in favour of supporting the government through a parliamentary agreement between us, if in the end of the day the party was going to divide part into one lobby and part into the other, I would rather call the whole idea off and lead a united party into a general election. We were all agreed therefore that whatever decision we took it should be a collective one.

There was another matter on which we quickly reached agreement. None of us saw any point in registering a vote for the government for that day only, to stave off an election. That way we should attract all the blame for maintaining in office an unpopular and unsuccessful government without having any influence over its future course, and we should also be exposing ourselves possibly to weekly "no confidence" decisions at the behest of the Conservative leader.

We therefore agreed that our decision should depend on the terms the Prime Minister would publicly agree in order to ensure maintenance of the government and on the creation of machinery to assist Liberal influence over it for the remainder of the parliamentary session. The rest is now well known. We took our decision, and I want to record a word of thanks to you all — especially to those of my parliamentary colleagues who had genuine and substantial reservations about the course we were taking — and to you, Mr President, and Geoff Tordoff as Chairman of the party, and many others for the necessarily speedy but efficient way in which liaison throughout our party was conducted. However history may judge the rights and wrongs of that decision, the manner of taking it was of a mature, decisive and democratic party.

Let me just say a word about the nature of the agreement itself. It is precisely the same as that we offered to the last Conservative Prime Minister in March 1974, namely support from the opposition benches for an agreed programme in the national interest. It is not a coalition. Coalition was not offered nor was it sought. In fact the Prime Minister and I have never even discussed the subject. Why? Because I have made it my guideline never to ask for things which I know it is not in his power to give. That seems plain common sense. But some people have quite fairly drawn attention to the dangers of a political arrangement which involves neither a coalition nor a subsequent electoral pact.

First, we are not inside the government and therefore some disagreements do occur after a government policy decision has been taken. This happened in the case of the petrol tax increase. Had we been inside the government we could have said: "Of course we agree with the need to conserve fuel. Let us therefore return to the system we used to have and which President Carter has just introduced of higher taxation on larger cars and less on smaller". As it was we had to get reversed a decision taken by Labour alone, a party which has very little knowledge of the problems of areas where a car is a necessary part of the cost of living, but on which we have extensive first hand experience.

Second, let's not exaggerate what can be achieved by the influence of 13 MPs on a party of over 300 MPs. Every day I receive letters — some hostile to the agreement, others friendly to it — which advise me to break it off if the government does (or fails to do) such and such. The list of potential breaking points becomes enormous. Let us face the fact squarely that "we are in the position of a body of men whose sole sanction to enforce their behests is capital punishment. There are two objections to that. You cannot inflict capital punishment for minor offences; and you can only inflict it once for any offence." These are not my words but those of David Lloyd George in 1931.

Now, at this conference it is entirely right that we should assess the consquences of the agreement. First, there is no doubt that we have lost some public support. Part of this was foreseeable and in my view inevitable in the short-run. One of the Tory commentators wrote: "The electors who built up the Liberal vote for years have been the electors who have used the Liberal Party as their outlet for protest when angry with the Conservatives". He is possibly quite right. But frankly I have never thought that there could be a secure or expandable future for the Liberal Party as a kind of convenient temporary wastepaper basket for the ballot papers of discontented Tories.

As to party activists, we have lost scarcely any parliamentary candidates or national or local officers. But we have lost some members, though gaining others. I said last year that the road I intended to travel would be a bumpy one and that we might therefore lose some of the passengers. Some of them must have had a pretty tenuous hold on the vehicle, for they fell off at the first pot-hole.

Our influence through this limited agreement has so far been largely but not unimportantly negative. We can and have stopped nationalisation; we can and did stop certain tax proposals both reducing petrol tax and freeing thousands of small businesses from VAT; we can and will oppose those cuts in defence spending which would take us below our obligations to collective security in NATO; we stemmed the flow of partisan legislation.

But our influence has been positive as well. Foremost, we have made a major political contribution to national stability and recovery over the last six months. As the director-general of the CBI put it earlier this month: "at least businessmen have returned to operating in a climate in which they can plan ahead — instead of reacting to circumstances on a week-by-week basis".

If anyone had said to you a year ago that in 1977 a Labour government would introduce a bill for direct elections to the European Parliament recommending a proportional system, you would have been right to doubt his judgement. Yet under our influence that has indeed happened.

Of course the actual system proposed is not Liberal policy and is something of a concoction, but it will be used on only one occasion until the Community as a whole agrees a rational uniform system throughout Europe for future elections, and it does have three obvious advantages.

First, the delegation we send to Strasbourg will become reasonably representative of political opinion in Britain.

Second, the system allows voters, rather than the party machine, to choose which candidates within a party list they prefer.

And third, because of the delays caused in the past by the uncertainty of the Labour Party's approach to the Common Market, it is the only way of securing elections in Britain in time to meet the Community target date of May/June 1978.

Of course we still face the difficult task of getting this system adopted in both Houses of Parliament on a free vote. It's a free vote for everyone and we shall be watching the division lists most carefully. We have a right to expect the substantial majority of Labour Members — and especially ministers whose continuance in office depends on us — to support the government's recommendation. We hope also that a majority of Conservative MPs will remain true to the European ideal and support it as well, though there are alarming indications of a readiness in some Tory circles to allow Britain to delay the whole European election, so great is their hostility to any concept of electoral justice.

We Liberals have often enough been the voice for European progress in Britain. Let us be so again. Our fellow-members of the Community are fed up with Britain always being last, always sullenly dragging its feet. That must not be the case on these elections. They must not be postponed as part of the British party game.

In a not so publicised part of her television interview with Brian Walden, Mrs Thatcher twice complained that in the February 1974 election the Tories had polled more votes than Labour. Well the answer to that is not to dream up another referendum, but to ensure that our system of election provides us with a government which commands the support of a clear majority of our people. That is the right way to strengthen parliament against forces which might seek to undermine its supreme authority.

Of course it may yet be a few months or years before we convince enough Labour and Tory MPs that this is so. Meantime the case for embarking on elections to new and non-government institutions such as the Assembly in Europe on the same proportional principle as every other member state is surely overwhelming.

Turning from the constitutional future of Europe to our internal constitutional future in these islands, it has always been the Liberal view that all-round decentralisation and reduction of government is desirable in itself, but we also agree with the reasoning behind the Labour Party's late conversion to the need for devolution to Scotland and Wales as a means of preventing the unnecessary break-up of the United Kingdom, a view shared by a minority of the more rational Tories.

The original devolution package was a mish-mash of two entirely different schemes for Scotland and Wales thrown together in one unhappy bill, with excessive veto powers over the operation of the assemblies by Westminster. The new devolution package which we have helped to create, while still falling short of the federal solution a Liberal government would introduce (and which enjoys increasing support in non-Liberal quarters), represents a substantial improvement; and this time parliament will also be free to discuss and vote on the case for proportional representation in these assemblies without opposition from the government. The long awaited aims of the people of Scotland and Wales for their own elected internal government can be achieved this session, thanks to our political agreement.

But the greatest gain for the country has not been progress on these important constitutional questions, absorbing also only to a minority, but on the new confidence and the path to economic recovery which has been followed with our support over the last six months.

Over this period the annual inflation rate has dropped. In the quarter before the agreement it was running at 18%. This last quarter it was down to 9.6%. The Financial Times share index has risen from 427 to 521 and earlier this month reached a record level. The pound has risen 22 points against the dollar after months of decline. The balance of payments has changed from a deficit of £76 million to a surplus of £316 million. The reserves have shot up from £5½ billion to £8½ billion and could be nearly

£10 billion this month. Meantime bank interest rates are down from 10.5% to 6% and mortgage rates from 12½% to 9½%. This means that the family with an average mortgage is now paying nearly £17 a month less for their house than they did in March.

In short the economic outlook is now very much brighter than it appeared in the spring. It was right to give the battle against inflation our highest priority. Rising prices have ruined the expectations of the retired, discouraged savings, harassed the housewives struggling to operate a family budget and forced many people out of their jobs. The relentless rise in British prices was also threatening to do permanent damage to our economy by wrecking our international trade prospects. The volume of imports was becoming larger and relatively cheaper while our exports became more expensive and difficult to achieve.

The stark truth is that from 1973 to 1976 we had successive governments, Tory and Labour, presiding over this growing threat to disaster and failing to rectify it. But in these last few months we have provided the political conditions in which it has been possible to start on the road to recovery. I don't believe it could have happened any other way.

But, say some critics of the agreement, that's all very well. So what if the country does benefit, what's in it for the Liberal Party? Isn't the Labour Party going to get all the credit as the next election? Having avoided the return of a damaging Tory government are we not now risking the return of an even more damaging Labour government?

Michael Foot is regularly quoted at me as saying: "What we want to do is to prepare for the time when we can get a full Labour majority again in the House of Commons. There is nobody who wants that more than I do."

Well he would, wouldn't he. Of course if a Labour government is returned at the next election with a majority of its own it will be a very different kind of government from the one we have now under Liberal influence. Read the reports from Labour's national executive, or watch their conference in this town next week. The onward march of bureaucratic state takeover and control remains their main aim.

It is up to the electorate to decide whether they wish to give them that opportunity. Let us invite the voters to compare the period of Labour government 1977-1978 when the Liberal tail wagged the dog to the period 1974-76 when the Tribune group wielded more influence than us. I've no doubt which will prove the more successful and the more popular with the electorate. It is up to us to argue forcibly and convincingly that a Liberal hold over government is both healthy and desirable, and that the electorate should seize the opportunity to increase our influence and representation in parliament. Our chances of arguing the case are stronger the greater the success we make of this agreement. We will enter the next election not just as a party equipped with splendid policy pamphlets and an excellent history in government in the distant past, but as a party which as I said last year has shown itself not afraid to roll up its sleeves and dirty its hands with some responsibility for the direction of national policy, and then made a good job of it. As Shakespeare's Henry V said on the eve of the battle of Agincourt "He that hath no stomach for this fight, let him depart".

The question is have we the self-confidence as a party to make such an appeal convincing? As I say, I understand many of the legitimate anxieties of those who questioned the agreement we made. But I am absolutely certain that the one course which would prove totally fatal in our standing in the public eye would be for us to be dithering and hesitant now that we have embarked on this course. If we stop now and say "oh dear, we've lost local elections and the polls don't look too good for us, let's pull out", we should acquire and deserve a reputation as purposeless incompetents.

What is the image of the Liberal Party to the onlooker? An ability to laugh at ourselves is not a bad political quality and I thought this description a few months ago by one political correspondent rather near the bone: "There was a time when it welcomed all and sundry. All the pied beauty of British politics was found in the Liberals. They were there to amuse, to entertain, to divert. All over Llandudno their orange badges proclaimed things were going on — a commission on microdevolution, a meeting of Gays against Fluoridation, An Esperantist coffee morning. There was street theatre, morris dancing and a lecture entitled Radical Alternatives to Sex".

Heaven forbid that we should ever lose the capacity to entertain and divert, and become a party of dull grey uniformity. But we do need a greater sense of professional determination. We can't go on lurching into by-elections with little money, no organisation and no candidate until after the writ is issued.

At the Assembly in September 1972 we had fewer MPs and lower opinion poll figures than we have now. Yet within eighteen months we went on to score our biggest electoral turnout in the general election. We can do that again and more if we set about it the right way.

The Labour Party in this country has been in steady decline for years. As a radical movement it is intellectually exhausted. The social democratic tradition has run into the sands and many of its ablest exponents have departed for more worthwhile or agreeable perches in Brussels, in universities or on television. The left has taken refuge in the reiteration of past doctrines and is making successful takeover bids in moribund constituency parties. The grassroots Labour membership in the constituencies has been shrinking steadily over the years to a point where a successful Liberal membership drive this autumn should for the first time give us more individual constituency members than the Labour Party.

We must give special effort to expanding our resources and that is why the Executive and the parliamentary party have joined forces to launch a nationwide membership campaign today. The response to my appeal for members at the end of each recent party political broadcast has shown that there are large numbers of people in all corners of this country who want to help but have no present contact with the party and are never asked to join. We must go out and find them.

What we have to do is turn the country away from the remorseless conflict of interest and ideologies which has rendered us incapable of developing and allocating our resources in a successful manner. For in persistent economic failure lies the greatest threat to liberty and democracy.

We have met together as Liberals at these conferences for years talking of the ways we would like to change Britain. Too often for us the light at the end of the tunnel has turned out to be that of a train coming in the other direction. This year we have done more than talk. We have begun to change — just slightly — the way in which Britain is run. Now we have to demonstrate that if this much can be done by a tiny band of Liberals outside government how much more could be done by a larger grouping inside the next government, and still more by a Liberal government itself.

The task of the Liberal Party is to convince people we need not be governed in a way which divides our people against each other. We need to face an election in which we argue that the voters don't have to choose between a government dedicated to making us all subservient to the state and one anxious to create a society in which you grab what you can for yourself and clobber anyone who gets in the way. Don't let anyone tell you that being moderate means being in favour of timidity or appeasement of the aggressive. I want our party to become the militants for the reasonable man. We need to create (and I shall return to this theme on Saturday) a nobler concept of the family that should be Britain.

Time is short. Our task this week is to prepare for that argument. Enjoy the Assembly. The responsibility on us is greater than before. But so is the need for liberalism greater than before and we must not fail our people.

David Steel's concluding speech was designed to lift the eyes of the Assembly away from the immediate pre-occupations of the Lib-Lab pact. He also warned of the future dangers of the new right's economic policies in the Tory party:

It was I suppose inevitable that this Assembly should have been dominated by the running debate on the Lib/Lab agreement. You will be relieved to hear that I don't propose to add more than two brief thoughts to it this morning. First, I believe that the press are in general correct in their judgement that this debate has added new stature and credibility to the Liberal Party. I believe that in the public mind it is going to prove much more convincing at the next election to argue our case for electoral reform through an even stronger hold on the balance of power in the next Parliament than we have now; and that by the next election we shall have been able to demonstrate not just Liberal policies in theory, but a first taste of the effectiveness of Liberal policies in practice.

Second, the argument between us as Liberals in the crucial debate this week has, as Cyril Smith rightly put it, been not about the ends which we all want but about the best way of reaching those ends. We've had a perfectly clear difference of opinion on the means. The vast majority of this Assembly has supported my view, but the minority who opposed it remain loyally united with us in our common aim of securing the return of a Liberal government in Britain.

I am delighted that the Assembly has backed the judgement of the Parliamentary Party, and I want to assure you that we in turn take serious note of your demands for more effective public presentation of Liberal successes under the agreement.

Thank you for your confidence in us. Now let's get out and tell the voters of Britain what this agreement really means. It is a step towards negotiated politics and away from confrontation. It is a way of saving Britain from polarised extremes of Right and Left. It sets the modern Liberal Party on the road towards the power and responsibility it has never known. We have nothing to be apologetic about and we have much to be proud of. We have helped to pull Britain back from the precipice of economic disaster. But I also recognise the limitations of the agreement. We Liberals have larger ambitions and hopes for our country than merely surviving the current economic crisis. We want to see fundamental changes in our society — and for those it is no use looking to the Labour or Conservative parties. We have to look instead to our own conviction and effectiveness.

If we really want a Liberal society in Britain based on the development of each person's full potential in a co-operative community, we won't get it from the Tory or Labour parties. You know that and I know that.

It depends on whether we can mobilise public opinion behind our radical humane alternative, and whether we can inspire confidence in our fitness to govern. Make no mistake, although we can achieve individual policy advances as a junior partner, the Liberal society we are striving for will only be brought about by Liberal-led Governments.

It should be clear to anyone who has followed our debates this week that the agreement is simply one between the Parliamentary Liberal Party and the Labour Government. There is no agreement, and there can be no identity of purpose, between the Liberal conference meeting in Brighton this week, and the Labour conference meeting here next week.

In this town next week will be heard the clamorous voices of class antagonism and crude Marxism. The heavy squad masquerading as the once great party of liberty and brotherhood.

We will watch weak-kneed capitulation to the intolerant demands of Trade Unionism — imposed closed shops and the extension of trade disputes by mass picketing.

The individual citizen is not respected in Britain today. Whether it be the way council housing is administered, or welfare regulations that confuse and restrict those they are supposed to assist or the determination to make life difficult for the self-employed, we see more evidence daily that the humble citizen is required to bow the knee for the benefit of over-mighty officialdom. It should be the other way around.

We believe in self-management and public participation. They, the State Socialists, believe in more bureaucracy. Their appetite is inexhaustible. If the proposals set out in the Labour National Executive's recent Programme for Action were to be carried out by the next Labour Government, we would be carried clearly over the thin red line which separates social democracy from state socialism.

And on libertarian issues too we are in a very different camp from the authoritarian left. We believe the Official Secrets Act should be reformed, and I understand that the White Paper the Government plans to publish shortly will reflect the wholesome influence of Emlyn Hooson and the Liberal Lawyers, who want to let the fresh air of knowledge and information circulate around the stuffy corridors of Whitehall.

Some socialists are at least frank enough to recognise the validity of our constraints on the present Government even though they do not like it. One constituency Labour Party Chairman put a perfectly fair democratic argument to me in a letter: "We clearly stand for certain things (such as nationalisation of banks, insurance and building societies) leaving it clear from the nature of the Lib/Lab arrangement that these will remain merely policy until we can persuade more voters that they want it".

It is up to us to dissuade voters on the merits of the case from allowing the return of a Labour majority to Parliament which would naturally be free to pursue such a course.

It is not the right wing of the Labour Party hawking their expensive consciences around, who have restrained the left. It is we Liberals. We have done more from outside in a few short months to reduce the influence of the left than the right wing of the Labour Party has done in a decade. Give us more seats and we can do even more.

But I say to the voters of Britain: if you recoil from the threat of the totalitarianism of the left, don't leap from the frying pan into the fire.

Freedom should be one of the great issues of the next election. British Governments, both Conservative and Labour, have been too little concerned with the implications for individual liberty of the continuing growth of Government control over more and more aspects of our lives; and of the undue weight carried by the great corporate interests of ownership and labour in determining the priorities of our society. Our commitment to a free society has always been the moving spirit of the Liberal Party: it is Clause One of our Party constitution.

But our understanding of liberty differs sharply from that of the Tories. It is time for Liberals to expose the poverty of their vision of freedom.

The new Conservatism deliberately rejects much of the mainstream

Conservative tradition of the last thirty years. The central emphasis of this new Conservative ideology is not on freedom itself but on the free market. Individual freedom is defined primarily in economic terms — the freedom of the entrepreneur, unhampered by Government interference. Its patron philosopher is Adam Smith, who wrote of a society in which the selfish instincts of materialistic men amounted in total to the common good. It looks to the Victorian age for its image of capitalism, which it equates with freedom. It repudiates the legacy of Macmillan, Butler, Macleod and Heath, the modernising Conservatives who insisted that the Party must have a social conscience.

In the strictest sense of the term, this ideology — Mrs Thatcher's recipe for Britain — is reactionary. Behind its intellectual posturing, it rests upon nostalgia for the simple values of an age which we have lost — and we cannot regain.

Adam Smith's prescriptions and those of his twentieth century followers cannot fit the complexities of our highly industrialised, urban society, in which government is inescapably caught up with industry and the economy, and in which co-operation among Governments is an essential factor in international economic stability.

I am not only concerned here with the illusions and contradictions of the New Right's approach to economics, but with the materialistic values which underpin them. Freedom does not begin and end with the free market. There is more to individual liberty than the freedom to pursue wealth without hindrance. The values of a civilised society — a Liberal society — must be based on justice, equality, community. I can find almost no reference to these values in the approach of such Conservative associated bodies as the Society for Individual Liberty and the National Association for Freedom. In their scheme of things, the good of the community, in so far as it is taken into account at all, is seen as somehow emerging out of the clash of private interests, without any positive effort on the Government's part.

This eighteenth century image of society, as a mechanism, its parts moving in a simple relationship with each other under the motion of the free market, may have seductive appeal to narrow logicians like Enoch Powell, or conservative economists like Milton Friedman. But it is entirely inappropriate to the problems we are facing in the last quarter of the twentieth century; and if under its new leadership the Conservative Party is so beguiled by it as to pursue their own rhetoric into a massive attack on those functions of government which operate to police the market, to protect the individual from the abuses of power, to create the conditions of liberty themselves for the vast majority of our population, they will re-open the wounds inflicted by the injustices of nineteenth century capitalism, and divide still further our already sadly divided society.

Nor is it just within the United Kingdom that the blast of the new right's contempt for brotherhood and community will be felt. One of its most pernicious and dangerous attributes is the indifference to the threat which the growth of racialism poses for us in a world which has drawn closer together in communication while drifting apart both in understanding and in wealth.

Tyranny, wherever it is found, from the Soviet Union to Uganda, and whether it be on the left or of the right, is the first enemy of Liberalism. But tyranny which is based not on warped ideology or the crazed thirst for individual power, but on erecting an entire fabric of society to suppress the mass of the people purely on the grounds of the colour of their skin is especially odious and degrading, for it denies the most simple and fundamental equality of the rights and dignity of each man with his neighbour.

Over these next few years Britain will have an unprecedented opportunity to take stock of its position in the world and re-order its own priorities. Thanks to the security and benefits of North Sea oil, we will have a chance to change direction for the better. We must use the oil revenue not only in the obvious directions of improving the standards of our health service, our education, the needs of the elderly and the public squalor of our inner cities, but to gear Britain for a post-imperial era not of grandeur but of civilisation, efficiency and harmony.

It is becoming a set political cliche to say that oil brings us unprecedented opportunities. The Prime Minister has called for a national debate. I welcome the idea, because the all-too real prospect is that the auction-room approach of adversary politics, with bidding-up, with exaggerated promises, will take over — and we shall be left in ten years time like a foolish pools winner, with nothing to show but a mass of debts and a hangover.

In our view, Britain should devise a ten-year national strategy plan to make use of the opportunities.

What should this strategy be? Apart from modernising the decaying fabric of our welfare society, as I have mentioned, there are three other potential components.

First, it should provide us with an opportunity to end the ceaseless alterations to industrial investment incentives, and allocate substantial long-term resources to the updating of industry. We should not resist the replacement of men by machines in repetitive tasks in mass-production industry. These jobs have often been soul-less in their requirements of the human beings who operate them, putting little premium on any skill other than patience and a simple dexterity. Their products often compete on world markets, which they should not have to do with unnecessary labour costs added to their unit price.

But we should seize other opportunities to expand employment. We should look to build greater self-sufficiency through food production in Britain, with farming acreage jealously conserved and even expanded. We should recognise that the petroleum base of agriculture, whether through fuel for machines or as the base for chemical treatments, is an insecure one. Long-term, the countryside should be revitalised, with more people working in what has always been one of the most natural of human activities — growing food.

We should look for an ambitious plan for youth employment. Instead of the present hotch-potch of emergency schemes, we should create a national volunteer service scheme, concentrating young people's efforts on our physical and social environment, and a greatly stepped-up training programme.

Second, against the background of new national income, the wholesale and radical reform of our tax structure as recommended by this Assembly can be realistically and speedily introduced. The Liberal Party has been in the fore on many policies in the past. We are first again with coherent proposals to lift the burden of tax on earnings.

Third, we should be prepared to spend some of the benefits of oil on capital expenditure to reduce our dependence for our future energy requirements on the narrow choice between further exhaustion of limited stocks of oil, gas and coal on the one hand, and our over-dependence on nuclear resources on the other.

Now is the moment to plan for the necessarily heavy outlay on such possible schemes as the barrages on the Severn and Solway, which would use the limitless resource of tidal power, as well as the development of solar and wind sources of energy. I very much hope that Mrs Thatcher and the Conservative Party might join with the Government and ourselves in the development of a national strategy for oil along these lines.

For there is a major threat to all this vision of a new prosperity and national assurance. It is the alarming lurch into more and more extreme confrontation politics.

A rational society depends upon civilised people arguing and reasoning together until they find a common way forward. The application of this idea to politics has been one of Britain's great gifts to the world.

It is all the more tragic to see in our country the drift towards polarisation, the gradual triumph of sectarianism. It is such a short progression from denying any merit in your opponent's argument, to denying his right to voice it, to questioning his right to exist.

It is hard self-righteousness and narrow intolerance that are the first enemies of civilisation. The bully-boys of the National Front and the fanatics of the Socialist Workers Party share this quality. So, regrettably, do far too many of the idealogues on the right of the Tory Party and on the left of the Labour party. If politicians offer nothing but confrontation, how can we blame those outside the system for imitating their example? If children grow up seeing their leaders engaged in an endless Punch and Judy show, are they to be blamed for thinking that there are only two sides of every question, and that one has to win at the expense of the other?

"LAW OF THE JUNGLE RULES, OK" ought to be chalked on the walls of the Palace of Westminster.

Great Liberals have always recognised that liberty does not exist in a vacuum. Each man's liberty depends on respect for every man's rights and obligations. People talk of "rights" easily; they talk of "freedom" almost glibly. Yet how often do you hear of "responsibility"? I fear for a liberal society when it is not also a responsible society.

Responsibility is breaking down around us. How can it be responsible for some Conservatives to treat one and half million unemployed either as second-rate malingerers, or far-away people of whom the well-heeled know nothing? How can it be responsible for the unemployment rate among black school-leavers to be two or three times the average? Are the screaming savages of soccer matches or violent demonstrations the product of a mutually responsible society? A great fuss was made recently about school-leavers not knowing the names of politicians. What is infinitely more serious is the school-leaver going into the world with no concept of duties as well as of rights, obligations as well as freedoms.

Free societies are based on mutual respect. Once that respect weakens, freedom is threatened.

I am particularly concerned at those who would use the law as a battering ram in pursuit of their own sectarian interpretations of freedom. Respect for the law, as well as respect for our institutions, rests fundamentally upon consent. If that consent is weakened, if divisions are exaggerated and conflicts pursued, then Britain will slide further towards becoming ungovernable.

The rule of law is under threat directly from those on the left and right, who abandon reasoned argument and take to the streets in pursuit of their aims. This imposes an intolerable and unfair strain on our undermanned police force, who are expected to act as referees in the midst of chaos. Remember that 1977 has been a year when the unacceptable level of political violence of Northern Ireland has spilled over on the mainland at Grunwick and Lewisham. Riot shields have been seen on our streets for the first time. But isn't it likely that those who resort to physical assault on the police derive encouragement from the verbal antagonisms of the more legitimate left and right within respectable politics?

There are those in the Tory and Labour Parties who would rather be locked together in mortal combat, dust and dirt flying, until one falls to the ground and the other is declared victor, regardless of whether they drag the country down in the process. The politics of the warring extremes is deeply destructive. It foreshadows the creation of the truly illiberal society.

Many of the right and the left would agree with each other that there can be no reconciliation between liberty and equality. But as John Stuart Mill in his classic essay "On Liberty" argued there is an unavoidable tension between individual liberty and social justice which only an active and educated democracy can resolve. Or as Schumacher (whose death earlier this month was such a loss to modern liberal thought) summed up our distinctive response in his book "A Guide for the Perplexed", it takes fraternity to reconcile liberty and equality.

May I for one moment be very personal? To be a Liberal in recent times can't have been easy. For each of you it has taken the sort of courage that can only be sustained by a great ideal. The struggle for that ideal involves many sacrifices, great commitment and a lot of patience.

I want to tell you what sustains me on what Andrew Phillips called the long march of Liberal politics. It is our concern for fraternity, for the creation of a self-governing society in which active consent is more important than the enforcement of law, in which participation is more widespread than bureaucratic control. It is a concern which runs through the whole range of Liberal policy. It underlies our commitment to devolution and the decentralisation of power. It is behind our attack on the obsessive secrecy of central government, and our demands for far-reaching reforms at Westminster. It motivates our enthusiasm for the co-operative principle in industry, and for the introduction of a genuine industrial partnership.

Of course it is not easy to reawake the spirit of community in Britain. We have to build a Liberal society out of the embittered divisions on which the other two parties have thrived.

But if we can harness the latent energy of the British people, if we can set free the imagination and determination of a people depressed and exhausted by governments which have offered them stone when they cried for bread, then our achievements can match our hopes.

Forgive me if for a moment I speak to those millions who have been following our conference on radio and television.

This nation once set an example to the world. It can do so again. But it will not happen without new leadership and a new generation. We are that generation. We demand to be heard. From now on we will not be ignored.

There is no power on earth that can resist an idea whose time has come. We are that idea.

To you in this great Assembly I say that in the last six months of struggle together we may have sustained some losses but we have forced a bridgehead. Now I urge you to go back to your constituencies and intensify the campaign.

This is not the battle of Britain. It is the battle for Britain; and it's the battle we're going to win.

1978

Chapter Three

A new majority for a new parliament

David Steel had left the 1977 Liberal Assembly in Brighton with some confidence. He was treading a perilous path perhaps, but in July had persuaded his parliamentary colleagues (some of whom were distinctly unhappy) to renew the Lib/Lab Pact for the coming Parliamentary Session. Ostensibly, the outcome of the Brighton Assembly had been triumphant. The Liberal leader, speaking at the very outset of the Assembly and thereby setting the mood for the week's debate, had crushed those calling for a renegotiation of the Agreement by a two-to-one margin.

But the seeds of looming disaster had been planted by an amendment to the Assembly resolution which spelt out the importance of Labour MPs supporting a proportional voting system for direct elections to the European Parliament. In short, PR for Europe had to be the price for the continuation of the Pact.

On the night of 13 December, the clause in the Bill dealing with PR was defeated in the Commons by 87 votes and the Pact was in crisis.

To be fair to Jim Callaghan and his Government they had fulfilled the spirit, if not the letter, of the agreement over European elections. They *had* commended a system of preferential voting to the House and, while it had not been substantial, a majority of Labour MPs *had* voted for the measure.

By the narrowness of margins, Steel persuaded his outraged and bitter colleagues not to break the Pact. But he agreed that the Special Assembly which the Party had demanded would have to be held as soon as practical. The Party activists would have to vote on the future of the Pact.

Not for the last time David Steel put his authority with the Party on the line. The termination of the Pact prematurely — and, in Steel's eyes, with dishonour — would spell the end of his political strategy. It would sabotage any hope of his being able to fight the General Election by presenting the virtues of 'pact politics' against a return of single issue government. Indeed, it would take away what he had hoped could be controlled descent out of the Pact and into the hustings and would precipitate an election on an issue of not the slightest interest to the British people.

The message to the Party was clear: if the Pact goes, so do I.

The scene was therefore set for an extraordinary one-day Special Assembly in Blackpool on 21 January. There was much apprehension and foreboding, as some 2,300 Liberal delegates converged by car, bus and chartered train on this windy out-of-season venue.

The Liberal Leader, abandoning his traditional speaking point on the platform, put the case for sustaining the Pact from the Conference floor. As Cyril Smith and those ranged against the Pact developed their arguments, it was clear that the question was not: "do we end the Pact" but simply "when?". As Steel put it:

> This agreement ends in July, anyway. The only question is whether we renew it for 1978/79.
>
> At the moment it is extremely doubtful that we would. I do not share the dangerously euphoric view that if you get inflation down to nine per cent you have achieved some kind of economic miracle. I do not think there is room for that kind of complacency.
>
> Nor do I think that if the Government simply used the North Sea oil windfall to reduce taxation without altering the whole structure of taxation in the way John Pardoe and my colleagues have proposed, that any substantial social reform would be achieved.
>
> If we limp on with a hand-to-mouth kind of incomes policy, that is no substitute for the real permanent thing that we have advocated. If you look at the statistics and see that we are producing less now than we did during the three-day week, I do not think we could go on to 1979 on that basis. If you look at the poor industrial relations, there is no point in going on to 1979.

Unless there is an attempt to move the economy to tackle the scandalous rate of unemployment there is no point in going on to 1978/79.

If there is no agreement between us and the Labour Party and the Labour Government on these particular issues, as there certainly is not at the moment, I think it would be better to put our different policies to the electorate and ask them to judge.

I reject the appeal of Cyril and others to end the Pact now and have a kind of 'on-off situation', day in and day out.

I do not believe that that kind of political uncertainty and instability would be good for the country, whichever government is in power.

We shall choose the right time to end our association with the Labour Government and we shall judge it on what is in the best interests of this country and of our own party at the same time.

Returning to the fray at the end of the debate, David Steel concluded with a warning to delegates:

I never said this was going to be easy. I am on record time and time gain as saying that if we pursued this strategy it would be difficult. I warned it would be unpopular and that we would lose members. I thought I had your support after all these warnings.

It is nonsense to say the party's lifeblood is draining away. Where's the evidence? If opinion polls show people believe the Pact is good for the country, but that they are not prepared to vote Liberal, the fault must be with the Party. Our fault — yours and mine — but the potential is there.

We will never project this agreement if we are apologetic and defensive about it. We have to be aggressive and positive. We will never project it to the electorate until the party workers themselves are convinced we are on the right course.

In response to cries of "No!" from delegates when he spoke of the possibility of renewing the Pact in July, he replied:

You must know that a week is a long time in politics and six months is an eternity. How do you know what you will do in July? How do you know what the political or economic situation is going to be?

I cannot talk in certainties, but the probability is that the agreement will have served its immediate purpose. We shall have inflation down to single figures, assemblies for Scotland and Wales, the European Elections Bill, and shall have started on the way to reducing the burden of income tax and started on legislation on profit-sharing.

Which is better, to face the electorate with a little book of detailed, worked out schemes, or with legislation on the statute book? It will be the first time that tax incentives have been given to companies for introducing profit-sharing schemes and not even the Tories will be able to claim that it is the work of the IMF.

I look forward to obtaining the balance of power at the next General Election, putting the thumbscrews on the next Government and opening the door to the introduction of more Liberal policies.

Whatever our disagreements about tactics, and they are natural in a healthy, robust, democratic party, let us be clear about our strategy; it is to get a Liberal government to create a Liberal society. That is what we are going to get if we keep our idealism, our radicalism — and if we keep our nerve.

David Steel won the day decisively by 1,727 to 520, an overwhelming majority of 1,207. Nonetheless, while the Pact had been saved for the time being, it was clear that its days were numbered. After the debacle over Europe the mood of the Party was critical and demanding.

This was understandably reinforced by the evidence of local and parliamentary by-elections which pointed to a distressing decline in the Liberal vote. In fact, in the ten by-elections of the period of the Pact the Liberal vote fell by an average of 9.5%, and in the Ladywood and Stetchford by-elections in Birmingham the Party finished in humiliating fourth place behind the National Front.

Finally, the economic indicators for the future were not good, and Steel had no wish to sustain an unpopular Government over what could be a damaging winter.

The Pact therefore ended in the summer, with the Liberal Leader confident that a general election would follow in the Autumn, and with the experience of the Lib/Lab Agreement fresh in the minds of voters.

It was therefore the case for coalition politics and the need for the Liberals to bring about that 'new' majority which formed the basis of his Assembly speech at Southport:

> When I spoke to you for the first time as leader two years ago at Llandudno I warned that the road we intended to travel would be a bumpy one, but I must confess that I never foresaw how rough it would be. Yet we lost remarkably few members and even gained others, and I want at the outset of this speech to say a very warm thank you not only to my colleagues in both Houses of Parliament and the party officers and all those who have been closely involved during this period of political innovation, but of appreciation and admiration to you all both in this hall and throughout the country for holding so firm and being prepared to travel together through these difficulties. Of course all parties must expect, from time to time, to run into political difficulties and we are no exception. But as we all know we've had other distressing problems as well.

If adversity is good for the soul, I think all our prospects of redemption must really have improved. At the end of a particularly long day I sometimes think of those lines of W. E. Henley:
> *'Under the bludgeoning of chance*
> *My head is bloody but unbowed'*

I am sure that all of us at times recently have felt bloody, but looking around I don't see too many bowed heads.

Indeed as I look at this splendid Assembly and feel the warmth of your enthusiasm, I think there are two questions which all the critics and Liberal obituarists ought to ask themselves. 'What is it that gives the Liberal Party its stamina and resilience? What is it that will see the Liberal Party going into the elections with high morale and even higher hopes?'

It certainly isn't what sustains the Conservative Party! They believe they have a divine right to rule. Nor is it that uneasy brew of class hatred and lust for office which fuels the Labour Party.

No — for Liberals it's something quite different. It's a burning conviction that what we believe in and what we stand for is right. Politics may have become a dirty word. It's prostituted and debauched by the way politicians bid each other up in an electoral auction. But it can still be a noble vocation for those with conviction and determination. And we have plenty of both.

Britain is badly governed. It is badly governed because its political institutions are antiquated and undemocratic. This crucial weakness is at the very root of Britain's continuing economic and social decline. There's no longer much dispute about this in the serious press, among observers of politics outside the range of the two establishment parties, or in the mind of the public at large.

One of the messages that has gone out clearly from this Assembly is that Liberals will not tolerate a slide back down the slippery slope of inflation. That's why we are insisting on a fair statutory prices and incomes policy. That's why we got involved with the government.

Yet we still hear the argument trotted out by Conservative and Labour spokesmen that the preservation of our undemocratic voting system and our impotent Parliament are necessary to ensure what they call 'strong government', and that any fundamental changes would lay Britain open to the sort of 'weak' governments from which our continental partners are said to suffer.

Let's just look at that so-called 'weak' government. Do they mean the performance of the German economy, or the cohesion of Scandinavian societies or the broad mutual tolerance which characterise the Dutch parties? Or perhaps they mean the way that new policies are introduced in other democracies with representative voting systems — the open debate, the careful all-party scrutiny, the search for a consensus to back new measures.

If that's what they mean by 'weak' government — I can only say that

Britain could do with some of it. We need a totally new parliament.

I'm sure it's satisfying to Mrs Thatcher or Tony Benn to contemplate the prospects of having the unfettered power in Government to bulldoze through their pet schemes. Satisfying for them — but disastrous for any prospect of good government in Britain. We need to spell this out to the voters in the clearest terms. Single party government, as we have seen it from Labour and Conservative is bad government. To get good government — of the quality which most of our European partners have — we must throw out our indefensible electoral system. We must give Parliament the power and the information to criticise and control the Government.

No-one in the Conservative or Labour front benches has found a consistent or logical case against a more democratic voting system. The arguments we have heard in the House of Commons in the past two years have been awash with contradictions. I remember Michael Foot saying about Spain after General Franco's death that he would not regard it as having regained democracy until it had a government which clearly reflected the wishes of a majority of its people.

I agreed with him but it didn't seem to worry him that he and his colleagues were totally hostile to government based on majority support until they were forced to come to an agreement with the Liberals. Tony Benn talks with conviction about the need to build a participatory democracy. But he shies away from the obvious conclusion that wider participation starts with a broader-based Parliament accurately reflecting the choice of the voters.

We've just had an excellent report on Parliamentary reforms from the Select Committee on Procedures. Lots of sensible suggestions which most people would agree with. Like most MPs I've had dozens of letters from members of the public since the broadcasting of Parliament started. They're simply stupefied by the radio rhubarb of Parliamentary debate, by what the Committee called 'the totally adversary character of present proceedings'. The *Economist* commented 'that adversary character is largely of course the product of Britain's undemocratic electoral method', and it was right.

I was astonished and saddened to discover during the Agreement with the Labour Government how firmly ministers resisted the idea that they should carry through their own manifesto commitment to repeal the Official Secrets Act. And I noted the strange silence on this issue from an Opposition which rarely misses other opportunities to attack the Government. True, Conservatives make brave speeches about the wickedness of the bureaucratic and secretive regimes of Eastern Europe; nevertheless they seem quite happy with bureaucracy and secrecy here, just so long as they can be in charge of it.

We have now in front of us a most scandalous example of secrecy. The record of the Wilson and Heath governments over sanctions for Rhodesia is deplorable in itself. British oil companies, backed by British Civil Servants, with the connivance of British Ministers and with the knowledge of the British Prime Minister broke the sanctions on Rhodesia. As a result Smith is still there, majority rule has still not been established, and Rhodesia is sliding into tragic carnage.

Since I spoke earlier in the week we have heard that the Bingham Report on Rhodesia sanctions is to be published next Tuesday.

I want to reiterate our demand for a Tribunal of Enquiry held in public to carry on where Bingham left off. I'm glad to see this morning that one member of the last Tory cabinet — Geoffrey Rippon — is supporting that call. Who are these Ministers of both parties and who are these Civil Servants who've set themselves above the law, who formed alternative policies in secret, who lied to Parliament and the British people?

I urge the Government to move swiftly to set up the Enquiry. Secrecy corrupts — and this Petrolgate scandal is striking at the very integrity of our government.

Secrecy, arrogance, resistance to change in the way Britain is run — we've had to put up with them for too long. And on all these issues the Labour and Tory front benches huddle together.

I've been talking about Westminster so far, but a genuine democracy cannot rest on a properly elected Parliament alone. We have to put the main assumption of British social life briskly into reverse. Tories and Socialists alike assume that people are not to be trusted, not to be informed and that they should be allowed as little real choice as possible.

By contrast the sort of democracy that Liberals want must be built on a structure of trust, information and choice.

That's why we want a Federal Europe; that's why we want devolution to the countries and regions within Britain; above all that's why we want decentralisation of decision to the villages, towns and neighbourhoods of this country. Power is like muck; it's better spread than concentrated in one place. The basic building block of a liberal democracy is a vital local community, with the power and resources to provide a satisfying shared life for its members. Unless the roots are healthy the democratic grass will not grow.

One of the other enemies of true democracy is the power that big money has in politics. A revealing table was published in the *Investor's Chronicle* a few weeks ago. It detailed the Conservative Party's support from large corporations and the Labour Party's from the big trade unions.

You don't have to be over cynical to suspect that he who pays the piper calls the tune. So the billboards have been full of Conservative propaganda, by courtesy of brewers and insurance bosses. And a bankrupt Labour Party, devoid of members and funds, has been bailed out once again by its union paymasters.

If you are a company chairman or a union general secretary you can certainly buy yourself some pretty high-powered representation in democratic Britain. With a bit of luck you might even pick up a whole Government at a bargain price.

Of course if you are just an ordinary private person going to work, doing your shopping, worrying how to make ends meet, it is a very different matter.

Is it really surprising that people feel alienated from a system where money and power get together to squeeze them out?

The results are obvious. Let me remind you of the Labour Government's craven acquiescence to union demands from 1974 to 1976, before we got our hands on the wheel.

The Dock Work Labour Bill and parts of the Trade Union & Labour Relations Act had nothing to do with socialism. They were simply a pay-off by the Labour Government to the Trades Unions.

I want to emphasise that Liberals have always supported the principle of free trade unionism but that is not to say that we go along with the worst excesses of union protectionism and bloody-mindedness. If Trades Unions are given their head by a Government which is in hock to them, we shall see more not less of this ugly and negative side of a great movement.

We Liberals must pledge ourselves to represent the ordinary citizens of this country who cannot buy influence through their wealth. Who will defend their interests against the vested interests of the owner party and the union party if we do not?

So the first priority for the new Parliament is fundamental reform of our political and electoral system.

But that does no more than clear the deck for the urgent issues of the coming decade. We are in the dying throes of the 'you've never had it so good' society. The plastic cornucopia is drying up. If we are to get our whole civilization back into a more healthy balanced relationship with the natural world, if we are to be frugal in our use of energy resources, if we are to find more fulfilment in our children than in our consumption patterns, then there will have to be profound changes in all our values and practices.

It's a commentary on the impotence of Parliament and the reluctance of the opposing front benches to grapple with awkward issues that this has not yet been examined or discussed at Westminster. Debates about economic recovery and future economic growth still largely assume that we can somehow get back to the easy days of the 1950s looking forward to doubling our standard of living every 25 or 30 years and thinking of economic growth in crude quantitative terms — as if the crucial problem was to get up from 2% to 4% and the long term aim to move from one car and TV set for every family to two.

I believe that this is not only a false set of assumptions, but also profoundly dangerous. Neither we nor any of the other developed countries of Western Europe and North America can or should expect to get back to the sustained and high rates of economic growth which were obtained for almost 25 years after World War 2.

In industry, in government and in life generally people are best able to find themselves and express their potential when they are not reduced to units in a calculating machine. Don't believe those who tell you that everything has to be big to be efficient, to get economies of scale. Cheap information-processing and high energy costs are making a nonsense of the monopolists' arguments. It's up to us Liberals to point the path away from the land of the giants and back to a more humane landscape.

Small is not just beautiful, it works better.

The Tories' changes in local government destroyed the one thing that really mattered — the link between local government and the local community. The baby was thrown out with the bath water. Since then many councils have been losing touch with the people in their areas.

It's the same with their new health boards and the vast hospitals that have replaced district hospitals; it's the same with the village schools that have closed; it's the same with the industrial mergers that may create new scope for highly-paid executives but destroy people's satisfaction at work; it's even the same in the trade unions where more energy seems to go into mergers and empire-building than into the protection of their members. It's the same with the neglected housing of our inner cities and their replacement by tower blocks and anonymous estates.

I want the Britain in which my children and grandchildren grow up to be more than a run down slag-heap, dominated by a few giant organisations — an urban wasteland in which all sense of belonging, of continuity between generations, of happiness, and satisfaction in life has been sacrificed.

We have had some some success in forcing Labour to face up to the demands of small business but that is no more than a beginning.

The New Parliament must face up to the priorities of the new age. A strong local community is the only place for the full development of the individual — and it's up to us to build that community.

It is a tragic paradox that in our rush to modernise and rationalise, we have so often discarded the very basis of a civilised life. A lively community, with its own local school and health centre, with good public transport facilities, with restored local buildings, with a local policeman on the local beat, with thriving local enterprises and a real sense of local identity. That's real civilization — and it wouldn't just be better in the countryside but in the run-down areas of our great cities too.

Re-building the local communities of Britain is a massive task. It will need some very fundamental changes in the way we do things. It will take a lot of work and I mean that literally.

If we really want to put people to work we have the solution at hand, in the regeneration of Britain from the grass roots upwards. It will demand a total change in priorities in the New Parliament. But it could be done. We could conquer unemployment!

We have seen the very detailed and impressive plans of the Liberal unemployment commission and we all have confidence that with the right training and retraining, with extensive re-structuring of work, with proper investment and above all with the right job creation strategy, we could take advantage of our opportunity to put people back to work. We could stop throwing away the precious resource of their talent and labour.

But it won't happen overnight. There are no instant solutions to unemployment which has spread like a cancer through the whole Western world, and is not confined to Britain. Any party which suggests otherwise is dishonest. The Tories are cruelly misleading the men and women out of work when they suggest that their queues could disappear as quickly as the advertising posters peel off the hoardings.

I was relieved that Jim Prior at least had the integrity to disown the ad-men's promises and admit that the Tories had no magic to make the dole queues vanish.

But I fear the taste for magic solutions which do not bear examination is deeply engrained in Margaret Thatcher's mind. Consider her notorious statement on race.

Two years ago I said — and you've endorsed it this week — that we should be prepared to join with other parties in the government of the country provided that certain basic conditions were met. I said then that we would never compromise with the obscenity of racialism.

Prospects of a share in government were remote at that time — they are certainly not so today. It is therefore even more important that I should make it abundantly clear that a fundamental condition for any co-operation with the Tories would have to be an end to the racialism that has so pervaded the thinking of the Conservative Party. Any immigration policy must be humane and civilised, based on the legal rights of British citizens and on human need, but firmly rejecting the criterion of colour.

Mrs Thatcher's views on the importance of family life seem to be strictly conditioned by the colour of that family's skin. Their new immigration policy would trample on the rights of teenage children to live with their parents; and we have never heard any hint of criticism from her lips of the inhumanity and degradation caused to the family life of millions of black South Africans by the hideous practice of apartheid.

Canon Trevor Beeson in his new book 'Britain Today and Tomorrow' says that the growth and renewal of our national character depends on us recognising the other face of society 'which is illiberal and degrading to the poor, the marginal and to the underprivileged alien'. We must realise that a vital part of our continuing duty is to ensure that our liberalism — which must be a passionate liberalism — affords every protection and assistance to all these.

For while the National Front and other similar organisations are crudely evil and must be firmly resisted, Liberals must resist even more strongly the more subtle, institutionalised racialism which is so insidious and which has become a curse in our land.

In concluding its submission to the Franks Committee the Joint Council for the Welfare of Immigrants called for politicians to return to discussing immigration, not in terms of numbers, but in terms of principles of human rights and family life: 'Only when politicians, in and out of Government, are prepared to take on this task of public education can the tide of racialism, swollen on years of debate about numbers and fresh restrictions, be turned.'

I have a feeling that the greatest of my predecessors, Mr Gladstone, with his deep abiding concern for the rights of oppressed and under-privileged minorities everywhere would have thoroughly approved of these words.

It's been saddening over the past 25 years to witness the gradual deterioration of British society, the slow decline in a feeling of the common interest which transcends the immediate interests of class, profession or pressure group. Britain is becoming one of the least generous societies in Western Europe. There is a sense of sourness and an unwillingness to help others which is spreading its blight across the country.

Politicians and political parties must bear a great part of the blame for this deterioration. The style and tenor of political debate does much to set the tone for society as a whole; and the style and tenor of the British political debate in recent years has been destructive and petulant. Politicians have play-acted at class war, because they believed that such play-acting would win them votes.

Oppositions have refused to give governments any credit for their constructive acts. Above all, both the established front benches have sought at all points to emphasise the differences between them — even when these are illusory — rather than the common elements in their approach. The result has been a general decline in popular acceptance of government proposals, a weakening of that popular consent on which democratic government must ultimately rest. If all these problems I've been describing are to enjoy any hope of solution then after the next election the new parliament must be wholly different in character and composition from all the post-war parliaments we have known.

What will be the choices before our people? An overall Labour majority? The Labour Party is not just bankrupt of members and finance. It is politically exhausted too. It offers nothing new for the next election. Labour has progressed from being the know-nothing party to becoming the do-nothing party. The danger which a single-party majority for a Labour Government would present would not necessarily be that Britain would be pushed into an East European type of socialism; it is rather that Britain would continue to drift hopelessly in the direction we have followed in the last fifteen years, towards a centralised corporate state.

Another possibility is an overall Conservative majority. They present themselves as a party of doctrinaire change, with their version of the capitalist society into which Britain would be transformed. It is a mean-spirited prospect in which all human values are decided in the market place with democracy as a secondary consideration and social justice a mere afterthought. What is more, it is false.

It does not fit the complicated problems facing an industrialised society in an interdependent world with finite resources. Indeed many of the best men in the Conservative Party know it to be false — and fear the consequences of Thatcherism if it is given its head in a single party Tory government.

When I first joined the party Jo Grimond had argued persuasively that Harold Macmillan's government could not possibly carry through the reforming changes which were necessary to stop the drift into decline until the chains of the two-party system were broken. Here we are, 20 wasted years of divisive government later, and Jo's conclusion is more than ever persuasive. Thankfully the Liberal Party is now far stronger, the stranglehold of the two adversary parties on British politics far weaker. Another push, another massive effort and we will break the chains, we will create that new majority.

The Assembly has helped to fill in the outlines of the Liberal society; our task now is to persuade the electorate that this is the vision which offers them hope. We have to create a new coalition among the voters, cutting across the lines of class, of industry, of regional prejudice and of race which now divide Britain.

Given the backing of such an elected coalition, we can then use the authority they have given us to make sure that any new government works to promote the common good, instead of following the dictates of ideology or of vested interests. Instead of tearing Britain further apart we want to start pulling it together again.

But if I am full of hope for this country and what it might become I am also full of anger. I am angry with the phoney war between the Tory and Labour Parties.

In the next few months the electorate will be hoodwinked into thinking that they are watching deadly enemies locked in combat. But Tory and Labour are actually the cosiest of competitors. As long as the Tory Party's turn comes round, it doesn't really mind the Labour Party. In fact it needs it! What else but the dangling spectres of Mr Benn and Mr Mikardo could get people to vote Conservative at all? And what a gift to Labour Mrs Thatcher and Sir Keith Joseph are. What would these parties do without each other?

Of course they don't want to change the system which puts them into power turn and turn about on the backs of their opponents' failures. They don't have any investment in Britain's success. Quite the reverse. They actually prefer a chronicle of disaster because it guarantees that they will get their turn at absolute power for four or five years.

That's why Mrs Thatcher in her speech a few days ago in my constituency declared that the choice of the British people ought to be confined to Toryism or Socialism.

This isn't democracy. It's rotating dictatorship. And the relationship between the parties is like an illicit market-sharing agreement. It's a cartel!

Mr Ronald Butt — one of the constant scourges of the Lib/Lab pact writing in the *Sunday Times* this week said:

'During the period of the Lib/Lab pact the Labour government was given something like security of tenure to do a crisis job. This it has largely done . . .'

Agreed — another one who's seen the light — '. . . Something more radical is now needed' — even more agreed — and then he adds lamely 'whether it is to be done in the Conservative way or the Labour way'.

They don't begin to understand that both their ways have failed and that we must turn to something new.

We are going to smash their cosy cartel. Why should we all have to put up with an arrogance which seems to assume the country belongs to the Tory and Labour parties? It doesn't — and the Liberals are going to prove it.

It used to be said that a Liberal vote is a wasted vote. Events since 1974 should have disproved that. I say to you that a Liberal vote at the next election will be the most effective vote that anyone can make.

We are not just another political party seeking power. We are the force that will allow people to break the pattern of national failure. We're radicals out to change a corrupt system. May this force be with you.

We have a candidate of our own for leadership of the next government: the British people! It's time they got a look in. It's time they took charge in their own Parliament. And we are on their side.

But don't expect to be universally loved for what we are doing. There is a heavy investment in the status quo by Tory and Labour and their powerful friends. Be ready for sneers and misrepresentation. But, whatever you do, never, never give way!

And if you ever quail at the prospect of still more hard work having so little reward to show for past endeavours, remember what it's all for:

> *For the cause that lacks assistance*
> *For the wrong that needs resistance*
> *For the future in the distance*
> *And the good that we can do*

and then the next election will be an historic opportunity.

Each Liberal vote and every Liberal seat in the new Parliament could be crucial. We cracked the old order and the old way of doing things in the last Parliament. Now we must break it into pieces.

This is a time for nerve and resolution. Let's go out from this hall and see that every voter knows and understands what a Liberal vote could mean for the new Parliament. An end to greed, intolerance and decline.

The new Parliament must be a new beginning for Britain. The Liberals are the only way to get it. We've now got extra time to convince the people that is so. Go out and use it.

1979

David Alton during the Edge Hill by-election.

Chapter Four

The high ground of politics

David Steel had expected the General Election to be held in October 1978. In fact, the Prime Minister, after allowing speculation to build to unbearable levels, announced that there would be no election after all, letting him know privately only a couple of hours before the fateful broadcast. The Conservatives, who had just embarked on an expensive advertising campaign, were furious. Steel, too, was annoyed. "The country had expected an election and will be disappointed," he said, "the sooner the Government goes to the country the better."

It was left to the Government to drift through the deeply unpopular 'Winter of discontent'. As the rubbish piled up in the streets and the dead lay unburied the electoral fate of the Labour Party was sealed. Ironically, and unfairly, the myth was steadily fostered that the Liberals had continued to keep Mr Callaghan in office in this period, and the Conservatives vigorously peddled what they claimed was this enduring image of the Pact in operation.

The Government finally fell on the night of 24 March 1979, when by a solitary vote the Government lost a vote of No-Confidence. That had not happened since 1924 and, like the election of that year, both the Liberals and the Labour Party were on the defensive against a reinvigorated Conservative Party.

The Liberals, bludgeoned by three years in which they had had to face scandal and humiliation, a change of leadership, the traumatic experience of the Pact and considerable electoral unpopularity, had one stroke of luck. Chance gave them a by-election on the very eve of the election — 29 March — in the promising seat of Liverpool Edge Hill. Local Liberals had long targeted the seat and their energetic and talented candidate, David Alton, who had already made his reputation on Liverpool City Council, had raised the vote to a challenging position through successive elections.

In a seat with a small electorate and with all the resources and enthusiasm available in a by-election, David Alton swept to victory with an 8,000 majority. The Liberal vote increased dramatically — from 27% to 64%, while Labour's support dwindled to less than a quarter of those voting. The Conservatives lost their deposit.

It was the start David Steel needed in what was always going to be a difficult election. Liberal support in the opinion polls immediately jumped from 5% to 10%. Even so, the nightmare haunting the Party was of the 1970 election, when a small drop in the Liberal vote, and a swing to the Right, had had a devastating effect on the Parliamentary Liberal Party. Seven of the Party's thirteen seats had been lost. Of the remaining six, three MPs hung on by the barest of margins — less than 1,000 majorities — including David Steel. No wonder that Jim Callaghan picked up a phrase first coined by David Penhaligon and told the Liberals that by helping oust Labour it would be the first recorded instance of turkeys voting for an early Xmas. The experience of 1970 was not one which Steel wished to see repeated. Nor was it, for by concentrating his campaigning activities in a limited number of constituencies, he helped his Parliamentary colleagues and boosted the vote in areas where the Liberals were already strong. By doing so, he also sought to demonstrate his main political theme — that the country needed to turn away from a system based on the debilitating confrontation of two ideological opposites to one founded on co-operation and consensus.

Steel was realistic enough to recognise that a Liberal Government was not in prospect. But a 'powerful wedge' of Liberal MPs in the next House of Commons could exercise a substantial moderating and constructive influence, as the Lib/Lab Pact had shown.

In the event, Liberal support rose steadily during the campaign to 13.8% of the vote. While that represented a loss of a million votes on the 18.3% the Party had scored in October 1974, it was a creditable result nonetheless.

True, there were casualties. Jeremy Thorpe, beset by his own problems, was badly beaten in North Devon. More surprisingly,

Emlyn Hooson lost in Montgomeryshire in a seat which had seen almost one hundred years of continuous Liberal representation. Saddest of all, John Pardoe, the Deputy Leader, was caught by regional backwash of the Thorpe affair and went out in North Cornwall. In what had been a Liberal heartland, the vote in Devon and Cornwall dropped sharply by an average of 9.4%.

Nonetheless, eleven MPs had been returned, and in 62 constituencies the Liberals had increased their vote. In Roxburgh, Selkirk and Peebles, Steel's own majority had soared to a record 10,000, despite (or as he claimed ruefully because of) his necessary absence from the division for most of the campaign. Equally encouragingly, the local elections held on the same day had produced a healthy crop of gains.

In June, in the first Direct Election to the European Parliament, the General Election vote was very largely maintained. On a 32% turnout, the Liberals polled 1,691,000 votes, 13% of the total. But the insistence of Conservative and Labour MPs in retaining the iniquitous first-past-the-post system for what was specifically the election of a representative Assembly, produced a travesty of a result.

With 51% of the vote, the Conservatives had won three-quarters of the seats. Labour, with 33% of the votes, had been rewarded with less than 20% of the seats and the Liberals, with 13%, received nothing. Ironically, the Nationalists with 2% of the vote, picked up the Highlands and Islands seat, where Russell Johnston MP, the Liberal candidate, was nearly 4,000 votes behind.

Despite this disappointment, the Party was in good heart and in reasonable shape electorally. Early indications from the two by-elections of the Summer — one a Euro-seat in South-West London and the other the Parliamentary division of Manchester Exchange — suggested a rising Liberal vote. Nonetheless, the Conservatives under Mrs Thatcher were back in power with a convincing majority. The events of 1977 were hardly likely to be repeated in the 1979 Parliament.

The Liberal Assembly gathered that Autumn in Margate, hardly the most popular of seaside conference venues. Nonetheless, when David Steel rose on the Friday to make his traditional speech he began by reflecting the Party's new mood of buoyancy.

> This has been a confident, united, inspiring and articulate Assembly.
> The Liberal Party is alive and kicking. That may seem so obvious to those in this hall that it is hardly worth saying. But I say it deliberately

because a year ago and throughout last winter and spring so many commentators were forecasting our demise. This Assembly ought to have been simply a gathering of the tattered remnant to put the corpse of the Liberal Party decently to rest.

The *News of the World* told us in an editorial in April that the Party would be "surely consigned to oblivion" in the general election.

The *Daily Express* told us in August 1977 in an editorial headed "The Liberals are finished" that we could not hold any seats.

Others more generously suggested that Jo Grimond would become leader of the Party yet again because he would be the only Liberal MP left.

In the last few days much of the press has changed its tune — they tell us that we may be poised for a great revival. Like the Trojans of old, "timeo Danaos et dona ferentes" — I beware of the Greeks even when they bring gifts.

We are poised for a great revival — not because the press tell us so, but because of the determination and hard work which we are putting in all over the country. Last week's Euro by-election in London and yesterday's result from Manchester gave us the foretaste of things to come.

The truth is that we not only survived, we did remarkably well in both the Parliamentary and local elections on May 3rd. Never in post-war politics has the Liberal Party emerged so strongly after a period of Labour government.

Just contrast the state of the Party when we last met here in Margate in 1972. Many of you weren't even in the Party then. We had lost more than half our MPs, had but a scattering of councillors round the country, and stood at 5% in the polls. Yet it was just after Margate in 1972 that our last leap forward started with the by-elections from Rochdale to Berwick.

We began this decade with a general election in which we lost half our seats and polled two million votes. We ended it with an election in which we held eleven seats and polled four million votes together with a remarkable number of gains in local government.

That result didn't happen by magic. I want to take this chance to thank all of you from my colleagues in parliament and the Party officers, to the constituency workers and the kids who delivered leaflets in the streets for the tremendous effort you all put in to the campaign.

There has been a further significant change. When I came into the Commons in the 1964 Parliament not one of our nine constituencies was an industrial seat taken from Labour. Today Colne Valley, Rochdale and Edge Hill, together with local government advances in places like Tower Hamlets are proof that the Liberal message has spread from Tory areas deep into the traditional urban and industrial heartlands of the Labour Party.

More important than our present electoral strength at the end of the '70s is the fact that the role and potential in contemporary politics of the Liberal Party is more understood and accepted than it has been for a long time. In my first speech to you as leader three years ago at Llandudno, I said that we could not build a solid political Party on the basis of being a nice debating society; that we needed to establish ourselves as the vehicle for change; that if we were to do that we should not be afraid to roll up our sleeves and risk muckying ourselves by grasping the greasy levers of power.

And we did. For eighteen months we risked our collective necks in the effort to help pull our country on to a surer path. We learned a great deal in that period, including a lot from our own mistakes. But we achieved a lot.

We showed that the Liberal Party meant what it said. When we made our agreement we stuck to it however rough the going. When we ended it and said it was time for an election we stuck by that too and defied the cries of "chicken". People know that they can depend on the Liberal Party.

We also demonstrated that when more than one political party pulls together for the country's sake it can be effective. Of course much of the Lib-Lab pact was drowned in the cries of anguish from the Tories and their powerful friends who simply wanted a Conservative Government as soon as possible.

Well now they've got one, and after only five months many of those who voted Tory must be pining for the days when inflation was coming down; when mortgage rates were falling; when industrial confidence was rising; when doctrinaire politics were kept in check; all of which happened during the eighteen months of the Lib-Lab pact.

People now realise that the Liberal Party made a significant contribution by putting the country first. We were not found wanting when put to the test. We stand ready to make the even greater contribution which will be needed from us in the future as the crisis deepens.

We stand for an end to the long period of national failure demonstrated by the divisive class politics of the two Parties. They have ruled and misruled our country for thirty-five years. We offered a glimpse of what co-operation for genuinely national policies could achieve.

But thanks to our loaded electoral system we once again find that we are back to one-sided partisan policies now that another minority has grabbed power. The Tories are determined to go it alone in the interests of their "side". In the face of that we should assert again that it is futile for Britain to go on swinging violently from failure to failure in search of success, from left to right in search of the way ahead. It isn't just that the pendulum is swinging again but that each swing goes further. The current movement to the far right will inevitably be followed by one to the far left — unless we stop it.

Time is running short. Each successive failure weakens our whole society. When the new Conservative policies of greed and grab fail, as they most surely will, the need for a credible alternative becomes overwhelming. It will be no use going back to state socialism and bureaucracy again. There must be a real alterantive.

And it is no good looking to the Labour Party to provide that alternative. No wonder they prefer to call it the Labour Movement for there is hardly any Party left, so great is their drop in membership. It is only kept alive by the life support system of trade union funds — and the price of that is the block vote.

They are divided between their idiot left and their conservative right. They're even afraid of such a revolutionary idea as allowing the whole Party, not just those in Parliament, to elect the leader. Now don't think I'm biased, but it's not such a bad idea, unless of course you're afraid of the result. A Party which cannot even manage to reform its own constitution is clearly incapable of reforming Britain.

A Party in decline imbued with the problems and values of sixty years ago may suit a country in decline. But those who want to regenerate our economy and transform our society will have to look elsewhere. One conservative party is quite enough for any country, but the brand of conservatism towards which Labour is slipping — protectionism, industrial stagnation and state control — is particularly unattractive and deeply illiberal.

The Labour conference starts next week. Contrast the mood with which many Labour MPs and delegates approach that grim occasion with the mood here in Margate.

Labour membership is declining. Ours is rising. We deliberate. They recriminate. They are introspective. We are outward-looking.

The fact is that the Labour leadership no longer trusts the Labour Party — and they have reason not to. Many weak constituency organisations have fallen into the hands of the sour zealots of the left. The right by contrast is bereft of ideas and enthusiasm.

I want to say this — not so much to Labour MPs and former Ministers — we all know that they have their careers to think of — but to the many people who have supported the Labour Party in the past as the party of conscience and reform. You know it is that no longer, and can never be again. Cut your losses — come and join us.

We share many of your hopes and ideals. The difference is that we mean to do something about them. We need your enthusiasm and commitment. And you need us if we are not to have a decade of hard-faced Tory government.

It is our job now to stake out the high ground of politics. There has been little affection for Mrs Thatcher in this Assembly, but we should at least recognise that she is a conviction politician. Convinced — but wrong! We have shown at this conference exactly the same strength of conviction except that we have nobler ideals of individual freedom and development within a responsible and neighbourly community.

There is a majority in Britain yearning for a radical alternative. That majority has not yet found its political voice nor used its power. Our task in the next four years is to put together this new majority — to offer the country a prospect of hope after the long nightmare of decline.

For a government to succeed in Britain it needs to be able to transform the atmosphere of politics, to create a different national mood, a sense of purpose, with three basic qualities.

The first is the spirit of co-operation.

A spirit of co-operation throughout our society is difficult to achieve. Yet we pointed the way in private industry with our introduction in last year's Finance Bill of the tax incentives for profit sharing schemes. The number of such schemes already in operation and in preparation already exceeds two hundred. As one city editor wrote this month with a note of surprise "at this rate of progress it will not be long before the company without a scheme is the exception rather than the rule".

The concept of sharing the fruits of increased productivity among the workforce should be extended into the public sector and indeed should be the basis of a sustained and effective incomes policy. Trying to impose a 5% limit on everybody regardless of the success of their enterprise as the last Government did in its dying days was a desperate and failed substitute for a coherent incomes policy.

The present Government has abandoned all attempt at controlling the inflation caused by unearned increases in wages. They say that incomes policies are unfair and arbitrary. That is just not true. It is certainly true of sudden and short-lived spasmodic incomes policies of the kind we have seen in successive governments. But no-one has yet tried sufficiently to construct a fair and continuous policy geared both to counter inflation and increase industrial efficiency. Sad though the loss of John Pardoe is from the Parliamentary Party I am glad that he is continuing his pioneering work in this field during his absence from the Commons.

There is no such thing as industrial relations, only human relations applied to industry. And they are appallingly bad in Britain. Whether it be in The Times newspapers or ITV or manufacturing industry we seem to be incapable of introducing new technology in a co-operative, efficient and commonsense atmosphere.

At Hunterston the new £100 million investment in the oil terminal has lain unused while two unions battle for the allocation of just sixty jobs. These are scandalous breakdowns in human relationships which as a nation we simply cannot afford and which sap our morale as well as our economy.

Here we must look again as Liberals at individual responsibility. It is no good waiting for the trade union movement as a body to reform itself centrally. Jim Prior is right to ask for certain modest reforms on secondary picketing and the closed shop but it is really not much use arguing endlessly with the central union leadership. They have become yet another group of out-of-touch bosses of giant institutions. The problems and the opportunities lie on the shop floor and in the branches. We need democratic and decentralised unions.

If you want a classic illustration of the difference between the Liberal approach to the greater distribution of wealth and power in society and the Socialist approach to the same end, you can find it in the argument which ended the Danish coalition government yesterday. The Labour and Liberal partners had agreed on the objective of greater industrial democracy and the sharing of profits.

But the Socialists wanted 10% of company profits to be set aside and paid into a fund to be administered by the TUC, the kind of industrial democracy favoured by Tony Benn in which corporate big brother knows best.

The Liberals would have welcomed a scheme rather like ours where a percentage of the profits of a company are made available to the employees who helped create it.

The objective is the same but the paths chosen have very different results. One leads to centralised socialist bureaucracy. The other gives people greater independence and involvement.

We must press on with policies which encourage the maximum of harmony and co-operation plant by plant. It is no good trying to blame a minority of reds under the bed for hijacking their fellow workers into hastening the downfall of a free society. The blame lies just as much with the manager who doesn't manage and with the good decent trade unionist who having paid his union dues never bothers to turn up to a branch meeting — or stays silent when he should speak out.

In housing, all the Tories offer us is the simplistic policy of selling houses to tenants. Nothing wrong with that in the right places, but far more serious are the human crises we have created, with private housing young couples can't afford, and with vast council estates administered from afar. Self-governing tenants co-operatives must be the key to restoring self-respect, control and morale in these areas before it's too late and we find ourselves having to bulldoze more than just tower blocks.

If we are to have a national spirit of co-operation the leadership, example and policies must come from parliament from the top as well as the grassroots. The Tories are just not capable of that.

The second necessary quality in rebuilding Britain is a new spirit of thrift.

I am glad this Assembly has made a start on debunking the idea which has dominated politics in my adult life that economic growth is an automatic cure-all.

The fact of the matter is that in a world of finite resources high rates of annual expansion in the production of manufactured goods cannot continue indefinitely — and what is more, even if we wanted short-term economic growth, we aren't going to have it for some years.

So instead of wringing our hands and saying "if only" — let's face up to reality and start to adjust our economic and social priorities now. For instance both Right and Left in this country have hoped that continuing economic growth would allow them to avoid the awkward questions of the distribution of wealth and income. It's time we realised that an incomes policy and a philosophy of fair shares are not just a desirable extra but the key to holding our society together in the lean years ahead.

A much better way of measuring our economic activity than crude calculations of growth is its effectiveness in using and re-using resources. This country has resources, natural, mineral and human. How well do we use them? — for waste is a real enemy of a stable and balanced society.

Let me take energy first of all. Each successive oil crisis, like the advance symptoms of a heart attack, gives us a warning. We are beginning to scrape the bottom of the treasure chest of stored energy accumulated over millions of years — and nearly exhausted by our civilisation over two centuries. In Britain we are relatively fortunate: oil, coal and gas give us a decade or two of extra breathing space.

So what has been this Tory Government's reaction? Have they treated energy use as a priority? They have not. They have cut back 20% of the pitifully small budget on research into alternative clean energy sources. They have relied on price increases to cut back consumption of oil and petrol. They have done nothing about conservation except talk. They only positive movement has been a rush towards nuclear power which fills most civilised people with gloom and foreboding. Mrs Thatcher seems hell bent for Harrisburg. She insisted recently on having her photograph taken standing on top of a nuclear reactor core "to show that it was quite safe". The national debate on energy policy does not deserve to be treated in such a simplistic and trivial manner.

What we must have instead of this mixture of inaction and rash impetuosity is a national energy plan for the rest of this century. It needs fuller information and democratic discussion but the main outlines are clear:

First a massive programme of conservation led and backed financially by the Government, covering factories, offices and homes. According to a Parliamentary Answer I received just before the recess, 60% of council houses have no loft insulation and 29% have unlagged hot water tanks.

Second, an expansion of energy-efficient public transport rather than its continuing run down.

Third, large scale research and development into clean and renewable resources like wave, wind and sun.

Fourth, a careful development of the coal industry as both extraction and burning techniques are improved.

Fifth, a halt to the dangerous and unbelievably costly expansion of the nuclear industry.

To develop a really imaginative plan along these lines which everyone can understand and play their part in would be a major step towards a thrifty and resource conscious society.

Then there is the basic question of food supply. The petro-chemical age of agriculture with its indiscriminate destruction of nature has passed its peak. This means that we shall need to employ more people in growing food and to find more productive acreage as well. I saw for myself on a hill farm in Roxburghshire last week how barren land can be dramatically improved. We also need more smallholdings and allotments on derelict city sites and, perhaps, most important of all, a halt to the seizing of prime agricultural land for endless urban development.

As the North Sea oil bonanza runs out we shall have desperate trouble paying our way in the world. Any responsible government must ensure that our long-term food supply is secured — with less dependence on imported food.

The examples of waste are legion: the elaborate plastic packaging, the derelict sites in cities, the flaring of gas on North Sea rigs, the queues of cars each with one occupant, the washing machines that have to be replaced because they cannot be repaired. But there is one form of waste which makes me angry above all other.

It is the waste of young lives in the dole queue. I find absolutely intolerable the attitude of free-market Conservatives who cynically see the unemployed as the necessary casualties of industrial war. Unemployment could even rise to two million next year. We just cannot accept that.

Of course employment is affected by the level of industrial activity, but it is affected far more by technology and industrial organisation. As Liberals we believe that more local enterprise on a smaller scale would not only provide a more satisfactory way of life but would produce more jobs as well.

And isn't it time we faced up to a shorter working week, not as a way of creating phoney overtime but to make us all shorter-time workers instead of having two classes, the employed and the rejected. More time to grow food, more time to improve our homes, more time for our children, more time for continuing education, more time for recreation, the arts or sport. These are all part of a full and satisfying life, just as work itself should be.

A thrifty country, one that uses and conserves its resources carefully and efficiently — its energy, its materials, its land and above all its people — could be stable and self-sustaining. A wasteful society such as ours is destined for the scrap heap.

The third quality required in Britain today is a spirit of common humanity.

In Northern Ireland the religious and political divisions represent a fundamental denial of that spirit. Since the problem of Ireland has bedevilled all British Governments in varying degrees for centuries it would be foolish to pretend that there is any instant solution. Our troops have been ten years in Ulster. In fairness to them we cannot contemplate a further ten years without any new political initiative. Sadly the recent talks between Mrs Thatcher and Mr Lynch appear to have concentrated on the important but in my view secondary question of security. If the men of violence are to be defeated the politicians must show greater imagination.

There needs to be a new element introduced into the situation which has become rigid, with all the participants including Britain locked in fixed positions. Our common membership of the European Community should be used to move both parts of Ireland towards reconciliation. If the European Community is to be more than just a common market, as we believe it must, here is a great opportunity for it to live up to its name.

Such a spirit is also glaringly absent in the field of race relations.

One of the nastier elements in the Conservative manifesto, repeated in the Queen's Speech, was the pledge to tighten up the immigration laws, odious and Draconian though these already are.

In July, eleven Anglican Bishops, including the new Archbishop of Canterbury, issued a remarkably courageous and compassionate statement. They openly stated that Mrs Thatcher's remarks about immigration "had the effect of fanning racial prejudice". The Bishops then went on to say:

> *"Existing legislation already strikes at the root of the family life of our coloured brethren. Further legislation can in the end only degrade the society which demands and enacts it even more than it does its victims."*

But the only response that Mrs Thatcher and her Government are likely to have to what Bishop David Sheppard of Liverpool has called "the hurt cries of the shut-out people" is to increase their suffering. But we in this Party must keep ourselves endlessly aware of them, and we pledge ourselves to fight unceasingly here for them and for all those who have no-one to fight on their behalf.

In an article written just before the election, Professor Michael Dummett had this to say about the Conservatives:—

> *"Their policies fill me with alarm, but it is their instincts that I distrust the more; their instincts are always to favour the fortunate over the unfortunate, the important and respectable over the down-trodden and those of little account. Britain under the Conservative Government is likely not only to be a bitterly divided nation, but one that can be counted on to be on the side of injustice in almost every international dispute, and will earn even more merited hatred for being so."*

All that Professor Dummett has to say about the instincts of the Tory Party has been amply borne out not just in race relations, but in the way their slashing of public expenditure cuts beyond the fat and deep into the muscle of our Welfare State. It was seen too in their belated and niggardly reponse to the desperate plight of the refugees from Vietnam and Kampuchea.

And what supreme folly it is to make the miserable cuts in expenditure on the work abroad of the British Council and the overseas service of the

BBC, at a time when we are supposed to be fighting the battle for the minds of men.

Even more squalid has been the cut of £50 million from Overseas Aid in the last Budget — to be balanced in exactly the way Professor Dummett describes, by huge tax reliefs to the wealthiest members of society.

Truly the Prime Minister has reversed the words of the Magnificat. She has filled the rich with good things and the hungry she has sent empty away.

So these three qualities are needed from our national leadership, a spirit of co-operation, of thrift and of common humanity. I said during the election that I believed neither the Tory nor the Labour Party was capable of solving the country's problems on its own. Neither of them is capable of adopting the sort of forward-looking national approach I have just described which cuts right across our industrial and social divisions.

Everything that has happened since the election has proved the point. Conservative policy has not been established in a spirit of co-operation, it has not shown a spirit of thrift, and it is conspicuously short on common humanity. Conservatism has very soon come back to its essentials: greed and fear. Greed for the powerful and pushy — fear for the rest.

If you earn £20,000 a year or you want to buy a villa in Spain or you are a speculator in agricultural land, this has been a good year for you. If on the other hand you are an average family trying to make ends meet it has got worse and worse. This winter it will get worse still unless you happen to be a member of a powerful union with an open invitation from the Tories to join the free-for-all. It's a far cry from the easy promises of that slick Tory advertising in the run-up to the Election.

So once again the national welfare is sacrificed to the ideology of one "side" in the class war. And yet Ministers keep claiming they have a mandate:

A mandate for 17% inflation.

A mandate for widespread national bankruptcy.

A mandate for higher unemployment.

A mandate for selling off our national assets.

Each successive divisive and dangerous policy is justified by this claim of a mandate from the people. It has a nice legal ring about it, but it is a fake.

Have the Conservatives forgotten that this Tory Government has less public support than any other Tory Government since the war — and each one of them was elected by a minority?

Have the Conservatives forgotten that their Parliamentary majority only exists because of a fraudulent and discredited electoral system?

Mrs Thatcher used to be very eloquent about the iniquities of Socialism imposed on the country with the support of only 29% of the electorate. Presumably her 33% makes all the difference. She should stop waving her phoney mandate at us.

She would do better to search for policies that have national support. But of course she will not. The best we will get out of this Government are some desperate U-turns when things go wrong.

It is more and more apparent that we shall have to be standing by with a genuine alternative, around which all the sensible and progressive forces in Britain can unite.

Right wing dogmatism supported by a public minority and backed by one vested interest is not going to succeed.

Neither can left wing doctrines backed by another minority and another vested interest. They've both been tried and found wanting.

It is only by collecting together a new majority free from these class interests that we will have a Government with the strength to shake Britain out of the long record of post-war decline and introduce the necessary reforms.

After the election I received very many letters. Overwhelmingly they supported our willingness to co-operate with other Parties in the national interest. We obviously struck a chord in an electorate which has become understandably suspicious of partisan politicians.

The willingness is still there on our part. But our electoral system again and again allows Tory and Labour minorities to seize power without constructing a proper majority for their programme. Time is running perilously short. The whole political and economic situation continues to deteriorate.

I believe that we must respond. In the past we have shown that we can be a responsible junior partner moderating extremism. But now we can and we must do more.

We have to be the basis for developing the political and economic alternative which the country so badly needs. We have to provide a rallying point on the high ground of politics for all those weary of the swamps. We have to accept that the gravity of the situation needs more than just Liberal participation. It needs Liberal leadership.

But that puts a heavy responsibility upon the Party. It means looking outward — it means bringing together men and women of goodwill, whatever their political persuasion in the past, who want to join with us in this historic task. We must be more than a Party, preoccupied with our own welfare. We must be the focus for a great movement of reform.

We have to bring together this new majority. All those who will walk with us on this road are our friends and allies. We must get organised. We must make them welcome.

We have to recreate the great coalition of idealists, progressives and radicals which supported and sustained the Liberal Party of our grandfathers. We have to bring together into one political movement those on whom the Labour Party has turned its back; the poor, the unemployed; the libertarians driven by opposition to socialism into the Conservative camp, and from the other side the moderates whose ideas the Conservative leadership has now decisively rejected. We have to gather in, as well, the trade unionists who want co-operation rather than confrontation in industry; those up and down the country creating new forms of co-operative enterprise; the new generation in the professions, in education, in the social services; and all those who care for our environments and our cultural heritage. Many of our natural allies are at present outside the boundaries of conventional politics, working in voluntary organisations, community bodies, and campaigning groups. I say to them: we are on the same side, let us work together.

This new majority is searching for new policies, free from the narrowness of class and dogma. New policies but based on old values. The values of freedom and brotherhood. They want a society they can be proud to pass on to their children, where every man and every woman can lead life to the full. A life in which the secrecy, mistrust and bitterness of modern Britain is banished — and fear is replaced by hope. We should not hesitate to be ambitious. This Party has changed a great deal in the last three years. We've learned a lot about hard politics.

Some people have still to recognise the change. A well intentioned editorial this week expressed gratitude that the Liberals were around because we would keep the Tories on their toes. But that's not our function. I don't want the Liberal Party to be just the political equivalent of going jogging.

Putting over the Liberal case is not always easy. Like all of you, I have an occasional sense of exasperation bordering on despair. It must have shown fleetingly in a broadcast interview I gave in the exhaustion of the day after the General Election. Suddenly I received an avalanche of hundreds of encouraging letters from some of you in this hall and from complete strangers outside the Liberal Party. I was moved. I was grateful. I was encouraged. I'd like to finish by quoting just one of these from a fourteen year old Manchester schoolgirl:—

> "Please don't give up now. Keep fighting. You can still win. I know I'm not the only one who is fed up with the insulting two party slanging match that goes on in this country. We rely on you to stop this and put us back on the rails. In five years I may be up there fighting with you. I hope this letter has not wasted too much of your valuable time. Lots of love to both you and your wife and family."

Then she added as a PS some words of an American President:

> "Nothing in this world can take the place of persistence. The watchword 'press on' has solved and always will solve the problems of the human race."

That young girl unwittingly echoed the magnificent call of W. E. Gladstone:—

> "Be inspired with the belief that life is a great and noble calling; not a mean and grovelling thing that we are to shuffle through as we can, but an elevated and lofty destiny."

My message is press on. Ours is a great and noble calling.

1980

Relaxing in the Borders.

Chapter Five

The coming brotherhood

The prospect of a solid five years of Mrs. Thatcher was not one which appealed to David Steel.

Admittedly, the Liberals could look forward with reasonable expectation to electoral advance. The Party has rarely prospered in periods of Labour Government, when disaffected voters have tended to switch sharply to the Right. But under the Tories once more, the prospect of the Liberal Party being the recipient of mid-term protest votes loomed large. All remembered the time of the last Conservative Government under Ted Heath when, from 1972 until the eve of the election, the Parliamentary Party notched up a string of by-election victories. Rochdale, Sutton and Cheam, Ripon, the Isle of Ely and Berwick Upon Tweed all returned Liberal MPs, and the local Government progress, if less spectacular (apart from the capture of the City of Liverpool in 1973), was substantial nonetheless.

Even at a very early stage of the new Parliament David Steel detected that there were rich political pickings to be had. Nevertheless he knew that, until that became possible, the attention of press and television would largely be turned elsewhere. Outside elections, little notice would be taken of a Party with such small Parliamentary representation, no matter how galling and unfair that might be. Mrs. Thatcher's majority was firm and her policies fiercely ideological. If progress was to be made, it was to be outside Parliament, chipping away at the electoral base, rather than in the frustrating atmosphere of the Palace of Westminster.

But it was developments within the Labour Party which promised to give the cause of political realignment new impetus.

Now out of office, its members (and the Left in particular) were determined that a future Labour Government should not repeat the failures of the last. In their eyes that meant the adoption of more than just a fistful of socialist policies. If these were to be implemented without evasion or betrayal, the power of the Parliamentary Party and of the Leader had to be humbled and the influence of Trade Unions and of the Labour Conference — as the 'Parliament' of the Labour Movement — had to be strengthened.

Inspired by the ideas of Tony Benn in particular, the Left pushed for change — for a new system for electing the Labour Leader, downgrading the say of the Parliamentary Labour Party; for conference control over the contents of the Party's Election Manifesto; and for the compulsory reselection of MPs in the constituencies.

Some of the moderate wing of the Party were deeply unhappy at these developments and what they saw as Labour's leftward lurch.

Unable to stop the vote in the NEC or at Party conference, they saw the coming Special Conference, designed to resolve these issues and due to be held at the new Wembley Conference Centre in January 1981, as the final opportunity for a last-ditch stand.

At the early stages many of these Social Democrats had not thought in terms of a breakaway, much less of a new Party. Some dismissed the idea outright. They considered themselves loyal to the Labour Manifesto of 1979 and insisted that it was the Labour Party that had departed from agreed principles, and not themselves.

Nonetheless a former Deputy Labour Leader, by then President of the European Commission and therefore out of active British politics, had recognised a deeper malaise and had begun to explore the wider implications.

Roy Jenkins's thoughts had matured during his years in Brussels, observing Britain from afar. He had talked informally from time to time with David Steel. And in November 1979, in the Dimbleby Lecture, he had produced a devastating analysis of the evils of the two-party system, had called for the introduction of proportional representation, and had spoken of the need to break out of the two-party citadel through a process of political realignment.

During 1980, the pace of developments quickened. A sprinkling of Labour (and Tory) MPs beat a discreet path to David Steel's private office, initially to share their unhappiness ('a shoulder to cry on', as David Steel put it) but, progressively, explaining the options open to them — thinking the unthinkable in the event of a clear break from Labour becoming unavoidable.

By the time of the Liberal Assembly at Blackpool, David Steel knew that dramatic events were near. The rupture might come at Wembley or it might come later — but some breakaway was beginning to look inevitable.

That much lay behind the scenes as Steel launched into his seventh major Assembly speech. But the course was clear — the aim remained a new majority, of radicals and progressives, but with Liberal leadership, a Liberal Agenda and Liberal commitment. The vision of the coming brotherhood was forming.

The predominant mood of this Assembly has been confidence. This has been a good year for the Liberal Party. Nothing spectacular, but a year of solid advance. It has been the most successful post general election year we have had in modern times. After each of the previous half dozen general elections the Party has gone into decline for a year with dropping by-election votes and slipping opinion poll rating. This post general election year saw our share of the poll rise substantially in all three Parliamentary by-elections, our poll ratings steady at around the 14% we polled last May, instead of dropping into low single figures. We had 76 net gains in the local elections in May, and in the four months since then we have won 15 seats in local government by-elections.

So the answer to Cross-bencher's rhetorical question in this week's *Sunday Express* 'Is Mr. David Steel brim-full of bounce as he packs his bags for this week's Liberal Assembly?' is yes, certainly.

I've long since ceased to be amazed at our pre-assembly press coverage. One popular daily in its editorial said we had 'become the invisible men.' Now in the last six weeks of the Parliamentary session the Liberal MPs launched three debates on major issues in the Commons, on the Trident missile programme, on incomes policy and on the plight of small businesses. In the first two the official Opposition stayed away. And how much coverage did the popular press give to our debates? Precious little. One of the more insidious features of life under this Tory Government is the way in which the efforts of journalists to report our activities are frustrated. With a peerage to a proprietor here and a knighthood to an editor there the popular press is seduced into slavish obedience to the Tory line.

This year Jo Grimond and Donald Wade each celebrate 30 continuous years' service to the Liberal Party in Parliament. What a transformation they have witnessed in the strength of the Liberal Party over that period and how greatly they have contributed to it; from being the remnant of the once great party of government (scoring only 2½% of the votes in a general election), to being the spearhead of a new and vital radical movement to change the shape of British politics.

In other words, Mr. President, the Liberal Party in 1980 is poised in better shape, politically, financially, organisationally, to make the breakthrough which we believe must come during this Parliament.

And never was the strong voice of Liberalism more required as we look at the state of Britain a year after the new Conservative Government took power. What I warned during the general election would happen has happened. But the nation — or to be more accurate 32% of our people — decided to take the Tory gamble, and how bitterly many now repent it.

The central issue in British politics in the next twelve months must be how to rescue the economy.

Each of the three Parties has its own analysis of Britain's underlying economic problems. The Conservatives see the problem as too much state intervention and seek to bring back a free market model of capitalism. The Labour Party sees it as the failure of the mixed economy and prescribes state socialism behind high tariff walls. The Liberals see it differently. Why when the world catches a cold do we get pneumonia? Our crisis is peculiar to Britain. It is caused by the failure of our political system and the inadequacies of our political and industrial leadership. That is why we assert, as we did in last year's election manifesto, that 'economic and industrial recovery can only follow from a radical programme of political and social reform.'

The Conservatives' management of the economy in the last year has been ill-informed and incompetent. They've said that their entire economic policy depends on control of the money supply. Yet in two months they've used up their own target of a year's growth in money supply and so their policy lies in ruins.

And Sir Keith Joseph was reported in the *Financial Times* as 'amazed' and 'incredulous' when he heard from his German opposite number that the German Government intervenes to support its own very successful industry. Here in Blackpool I met a deputation of workers from the apparently doomed Bowater newsprint plant at Ellesmere Port. It isn't just a case of losing 1500 jobs directly and up to 5000 indirectly because of this closure. If it goes ahead it will mean that in future only 4% of our country's newsprint will be made in Britain. Why? Partly because their competitors in Canada and Sweden have governments who believe in cheap energy prices for industry. Our own Government's slavish attachment to non-intervention is directly and permanently destroying parts of our economy.

They have been selling off our public assets and closing down the private ones. A few years ago Ted Heath described asset stripping as 'the unacceptable face of capitalism'. I tell you where you'll find the nation's asset strippers now — round the Cabinet table in No. 10. How many

Conservatives today faced with these grim economic theorists must sigh for the days when a Tory Prime Minister sat in a corner playing quietly with his matchsticks. At least Sir Alec never threatened to burn down the house.

The Labour alternative, of more public ownership and increased state control, is only the reassertion of an old solution which has failed before. They put all our problems down to the failings of the Keynesian mixed economy. That's astonishingly parochial. Has the mixed economy failed in Germany, or in France, or in Holland? Of course not.

I believe that in the long run, we will not reverse Britain's economic and industrial decline without far-reaching political change. That's why a more democratic Parliament and a more open political system are central planks in the Liberal platform.

But our immediate problems in Britain are so severe that their redress must start alongside political reform.

We need an urgent programme of the kind called for at this Assembly to tackle unemployment. It will need positive government measures, not lectures. The Prime Minister's response to the unemployed in South Wales — let them move house — deserves to go down in history alongside 'let them eat cake' as one of the most callous failures by those in power to understand the problems of ordinary people.

Time and again when I look at Mrs. Thatcher's personal direction of the policies of this government she reminds me of a First World War general. She has the determination to pursue her objectives at whatever human cost, and to go on pursuing them as the casualties mount and in defiance of all the evidence that the strategy has collapsed. It's not her courage that I question. It's simply her judgement.

All of us politicians naturally draw heavily on our own personal experience of life, but we have an obligation to examine and try to understand and sympathise with those who endure difficulties we never had ourselves. Because Mrs. Thatcher had the good fortune and undoubted ability to transform herself from a prosperous grocer's daughter in Grantham to an even more prosperous barrister in Chelsea does not mean that most of the nation can live the same way. How can she say to the unemployed school leavers on the street corners in Liverpool 'you've priced yourselves out of a market'? How can she grasp the very different problems of the one-parent families, the racially persecuted, the disabled or the squalor of our overcrowded prisons? She cannot understand them because they fall outside her own narrow experience of life.

In a penetrating analysis a few months ago the *Scotsman* journalist Julie Davidson wrote: 'When I asked her if she would feel any sense of historical responsibility towards women as the first woman Prime Minister she pondered politely then said: 'I think it will do a great deal for women at the top'. Not women at the bottom, or in the middle, take note, but women like Mrs. Thatcher, dedicated meritocrats, who feel that there is no special disadvantage in being poor, black or female.'

Liberals reject such an attitude. While of course encouraging the strong, we believe it to be the duty of the Government to intervene to protect the life of all its citizens as skilfully as possible. In the short run the Government must adopt a programme to cut unemployment and revive our sick economy without feeding inflation. We demand action immediately in six areas:

First, increase public investment where jobs will result and at the same time our basic infrastructure could be improved, for example, in the track and rolling stock of British Rail, in selective road by-pass building, in insulating houses and offices, in the coal board, and in a trial tidal barrage scheme such as the Severn to produce pollution-free power.

Second, cut the level of the pound by reducing the bank rate and help business by introducing a two tier interest rate. If she won't listen to small business, at least let her listen to the CBI today.

Third to encourage more youth employment, cut the employers' national insurance contribution for all those employed under the age of 21 and greatly expand both the public and private industry training programmes.

Fourth, start a 'Buy British' campaign and give the lead by legislating this session for the clear marking of the country of origin of all imported goods.

Fifth create without delay the machinery for a sustained policy on prices and income increases, including a rapid expansion of profit sharing schemes throughout industry.

Sixth construct in every local authority area new plants to recycle and re-use waste materials such as metal, paper and glass.

All of this is short term and immediate and it will require some government expenditure. But it will be much less wasteful than the 8 billion pounds which our present 2 million unemployed are costing the exchequer. It is a far better and more constructive alternative to the do nothing policies of the present government.

We've heard a lot of loose and dangerous talk from both left and right in the past year about 'conviction politics', the need for confrontation and the end of consensus. Both sides insist, in extreme language, that there is *no* alternative to their policies — monetarist or marxist.

I want to remind you and them of the underlying principles upon which democratic politics must be founded. Democratic government must rest upon consent. Governments should persuade, not bully. This Government did not gain the consent of a majority at the ballot box. All the more reason to try and find policies which command public support.

Yet like the last Labour Government, the Conservatives have hastily tried to bulldoze their manifesto proposals through within their first year — refusing consultation or compromise.

What every democrat should really object to is the Government's explicit rejection of persuasion and compromise as a way of carrying the electors along with its policies. In Venice the Prime Minister said 'dialogue is not a word I like very much'. That's the problem. We have a Government which hectors — and an electorate which has decided not to listen. Every PM dictates the style of his or her administration. In this respect I noted with interest the comments of the interviewer at ICI at Runcorn in 1948 who rejected the lady in her application for a job. 'This woman is headstrong, obstinate, and dangerously self-opinionated'. I must confess to a sneaking admiration for anyone who can remain utterly consistent over 30 years.

This passion for confrontation in politics and industry is destructive and dangerous. It threatens to tear apart our social and economic fabric. The logic is inescapable. Violent language eventually provokes violent action. If government by consent is deliberately ruled out all that remains is government by coercion. The fine rhetoric of Tory spokesmen on law and order could turn bitter in their mouths if their political intolerance and economic callousness end up provoking direct action and protest on the streets.

It is one of the worst evils of our political structure that it has encouraged such intolerance, to a point where in both the established Parties 'moderation' is considered weakness, 'reform' useless — where ministers and opposition spokesmen now talk loosely of revolution and counter-revolution.

Democratic government depends upon a careful balance between the three fundamental principles of liberty, equality and fraternity. This has been the core of the Liberal tradition, the basis for the consensus of liberal democracy which the ideologues of the Conservative and Labour Parties would now like Britain to reject.

The Conservative Party claims to be committed to liberty above all. But theirs is a narrow and crabbed view of liberty, confined to economic freedom and the removal of the government's protective role in helping the poor and underprivileged. This new Conservatism explicitly rejects any concern for social justice and equality, any element of compassion for those not tough enough or lucky enough to survive in their Darwinian world.

This ludicrous pre-occupation with the economic theories of last century completely ignores the positive role of the modern civilised state in providing what the Liberal Party Constitution calls the 'conditions of liberty', the freedom from want and from fear which Conservative policies are doing their best to recreate.

Therein lies the basic fallacy of the new Conservative economics. It is a Victorian philosophy fitted only for a Victorian age. The free market philosophers did not have to cope with a world so dependent on oil that it is dislocated when OPEC bumps up oil prices; in which there are huge industrial corporations, many of them multi-national; in which trade unions have monopoly bargaining power; in which most governments subsidize food production; in which many governments produce deliberate cheap energy policies for their industries against whom we have to compete. That is the real world of the 1980s. Britain requires a government whose policies face today's realities, not one which pretends they don't exist because the facts are inconsistent with their theories.

Of course, there is an acceptable alternative to present Government philosophy — but it is not found in the official Opposition. The Labour Party emphasises its commitment to equality. A narrow view of equality, by and large, imposed and administered by central government. Labour politicians generally show less and less concern for liberty as a principle which must temper the pursuit of equality. Theirs was the Government which included a freedom of information bill in their manifesto; then in office they entirely concealed from Parliament and people their expensive decision to upgrade Polaris. The Tories have merely followed with the monstrous extravagance of the Trident missile proposals. The Labour Party's approach to public housing, to education, to trade unions and industrial relations, all place a high value on collective uniformity and bureaucratic control and pay little attention to individual wishes or the right of minorities to dissent.

Their attitude to representative democracy itself is ambivalent and restrictive, both within their own Party, and in their resistance to all constitutional reforms except abolishing the second chamber. Their national executive's mid-term manifesto actually proposes a general nationalisation enabling act which would allow any future Labour minister to nationalise any industry by parliamentary order in an hour and a half.

Many in the Labour Party are waiting to see what will happen at their conference. If the left further entrench their takeover some will find it no longer possible to stay. But I predict that that is not what will happen. Rather I believe that there will be a fudged compromise allowing the left to continue its attempts to control the Labour Party while those of publicly proclaimed tender conscience will be enabled to remain within it in the hope of picking up places in the next Labour cabinet. All of this will be achieved by the undemocratic device of the Trade Union block vote at the conference. This will increase still further the financial and political hold which a handful of trade union leaders would have over any future Labour government.

As Mr. Terry Duffy put it succinctly a few weeks ago, speaking of the divide among politicians in the Labour Party: 'At the end of the day the politicians have to remember that the unions are the paymasters — we pay the bill.'

How appropriate that the Labour Party's national executive should propose that the Trades Unions should have 50% of the votes in a new electoral college to elect the party leader. Why not give them 100% and recognise the reality that the Labour Party is becoming their wholly owned subsidiary?

At the TUC conference Mr. Callaghan called for the co-operation of the trade union movement in a prices and incomes policy for five years. Now I share his view of the need for such a policy, and of course any sensible government will seek the co-operation of the trade unions in it. But what is not tolerable in a free democratic society is that the contents of such a policy should be dictated by, or vetoed by, any one organisation in the state, however powerful. A Government representing a majority of the people and responsible to a freely elected parliament must be the final authority on any such policy.

But the Labour Party is now in hock and that is why I believe that whatever happens at the forthcoming Labour conference the result will be profoundly illiberal and unacceptable.

Neither of the two adversary parties cares much at all for fraternity. The *Sunday Telegraph* comparing Mrs. Thatcher to Ronald Reagan, rhapsodized on how each derived their strength and support from the expanding South, rejecting the urban and industrial areas of the North in their respective countries. What a way to divide Britain; to recreate two nations. As for Labour — the pursuit of the class war, with brotherhood for some and hostility for the rest, is becoming a more and more central part of the Socialist orthodoxy. And for both parties, brotherhood stops at the water's edge. Labour's deep veins of chauvinism and xenophobia come to the surface in their suspicions of everything European; while the Conservatives embrace Europe only at the expense of the Third World and the problem of world poverty.

The inhuman and niggardly reaction of this government to the far reaching proposals of the Brandt report is not just a national but a global scandal. Our performance at the current UN special assembly on world development has been shameful and alone among EEC countries. We are reducing our aid at a time the plight of the Third World is growing worse. But how can we expect a party which fails to practise brotherhood in this country to extend it elsewhere?

We have incorporated into our legislative system discrimination which is blatantly and solely based on the colour of a person's skin; legislation which divides families, separates elderly parents from their children, discriminates against coloured British women as opposed to white British women, and then the Home Secretary talks about everyone lawfully here being treated equally and the Conservatives prate about the sanctity of family life. This is hypocritical and they know it.

Obnoxious legislation is enacted and people like the wretched Filipino women workers soon find themselves in some technical breach of it. The government is making things worse by publishing a nationality white paper extending institutionalised racialism still further.

This institutionalised racialism now pervades the whole field of race relations. Thanks to the infamous 1971 Immigration Act, the police have power to question and arrest anyone whom they suspect of being an illegal immigrant — this has led to the notorious fishing expeditions where British citizens, lawfully settled here for many years, find themselves in police cells until, and sometimes even after, they have produced their passports or other documents.

Mr. Whitelaw may say that there is no need for any coloured person to carry his passport, but faced with the humiliating possibility of questioning, many now feel obliged to do so. A West London magistrate last month made adverse comment on the fact that a 22 year old student was arrested at 3 o'clock in the morning and wrongly held in custody for three days because of a mistake on a Home Office computer. This is a disgrace in a civilised community.

Now in spite of an all-Party recommendation to do so the Government is trying to wriggle out of abolishing the SUS laws. These are harmful both to community relations and to the image of the police, for whom it is utterly wrong to have such power.

We have heard a great deal in recent weeks about the right of free speech in connection with National Front marches. The right of free speech is one which is very dear and rightly so to all Liberals, but there is a right that must be dearer, and that is the right of minorities, already under severe pressure, to live peacefully in their homes without having Neo-Fascist bully boys escorted by the police marching past their homes shouting their hate-filled slogans and terrifying their wives and children.

That is not free speech — that is Nazism and must be resisted by applying all the legislation that exists to ban such provocative activities, so that the terrible experience of Southall is never repeated. And to those who would say that this is not being liberal I would say that we have to avoid the danger of being tolerant in principle when other people are paying the price in terms of human suffering.

But what can we expect of a Government led by someone who draws from the parable of the Good Samaritan the somewhat novel interpretation — and I quote her exact words: 'No one would remember the Good Samaritan if he'd only had good intentions — he had money as well'.

The parable of the Good Samaritan is nothing to do with money — it is about a despised outsider showing love and compassion when supposedly respectable pillars of the community pass by on the other side.

Let her try to understand the real lesson of the parable instead of trying to adapt it to her crudely materialistic political philosophy.

There is a better and more wholesome alternative, and to all members of the ethnic minorities so cruelly intimidated and harrassed I pledge my total and utter support, and that of every Liberal. We shall fight the obscenity of racialism wherever it presents itself inside Parliament or outside it.

For Liberals, liberty can only be achieved within the context of a free and open society, in which there are no extremes of wealth or poverty, nor deep divisions of class, or religion, or race or creed.

A constructive political leadership would work to generate popular consent, to bring people together; to change people's attitudes so that we can transform society. The Conservative and Labour leaderships are both turning their backs on these democratic truths. So it falls to the Liberal party to reassert them, to bring them home to the electorate, and to persuade the men and women of Britain that this is the only basis which offers our impoverished and battered society hope for the future.

That's why I welcomed the time and attention the Liberal Party has spent debating the foundation of our beliefs. It is right for a democratic party to step back, in the aftermath of a general election, to examine its values and their relevance to current problems, as a preparation for the next campaign. I'm happy that we're able to do so constructively, rather than indulging in destructive infighting like the Labour Party.

So there *is* an alternative, not just to the present Government but to a discredited system of politics.

The question is 'How do we achieve it?' Or rather how do the people of Britain succeed in getting the alternative we so desperately need to the bankrupt policies of the past?

I have no doubt that there is a substantial majority of our people in favour of the principles and policies I have outlined. We have to release that majority from the traps of the two doctrinaire parties in which they have been ensnared. We have to turn the commonsense majority into a new electoral majority.

It will not be easy, but I believe our fate as a nation depends on it. It is *our* Party, the Liberal Party, which holds the key. It is *we* who have to call into being a whole new world of politics to redress the balance of the old. *To all those of whatever persuasion who share our analysis we should wish success in their courageous efforts to break up the monoliths of the old parties. But they should also know that without Liberal leadership, a Liberal agenda and Liberal commitment their efforts are doomed. The trail of British politics is littered with the skeletons of well-intentioned breakaway groups who tried to go it alone. With us they could make a formidable contribution. Without us they will perish.*

We Liberals must develop our policies and put them forward vigorously as an alternative to the folly of this government. The Tories say they will not change course but when they are heading straight for the rocks we say they must change course — *even if it means dropping the pilot*. Every parliamentary and council by-election must give them the same message. In particular the county council elections next year are the opportunity for people to demand a new future by electing more Liberals than ever before. Tory policies can and must be changed.

But that in itself will be no more than another last-minute escape from disaster. Any long-term success for Britain depends on a far more fundamental change to our politics. It depends on stopping the ever more frantic swing between the two ever more desperate extremes. As John Stuart Mill wrote: 'When society requires to be rebuilt, there is no use in attempting to rebuild it on the old plan'.

That is why this Party must be more ambitious and self-confident than ever before. We must be able to offer the country at the next general election not just a Liberal minority influence but the prospect of a new government which will break this unrepresentative and divisive two party dictatorship once and for all.

We intend to change the system of elections and government so that power is taken away from these two arrogant parties and put back where it belongs in a democracy, in the hands of the people. We intend to reform industry too so that what is now a bitter battlefield becomes a prosperous partnership.

Prime Minister, *here* is the alternative to what you are doing to our country.

These are ambitious aims. It will need an effective, well-organised and adequately financed Party to realise them.

To members of other Parties I want to say this. Break free from the past. It's time to think of the future. We need your help. Come and join us in this great task. We need many more thousands of enthusiastic workers and many more million voters. You could be one of them — and you could help find a new start for Britain working with us.

To Liberals I say: go out and find new members and supporters and welcome them in. We must have an open door policy. I want to be quite candid with you. People are fed up with political parties. They hate the exaggerated promises and the easy way they are broken. They think the parties are narrow, smug and self-satisfied. They don't believe in parties who say 'we alone have all the answers', parties who are suspicious of newcomers. We must never be like that. We've got to be different.

While I want the Liberal Party now to be more ambitious, let us not be so arrogant and purist towards others who have come to share our vision of what could and should be that we behave like an exclusive club rather than give the lead to a broad radical movement. We must recognise that most of those who will join with us will have supported other parties in the past. Like many people in this hall they will have trod the hard path of disillusionment. It is up to us to give them hope — and the welcome to go with it.

Let us say boldly to the people of our country at the next election:
> 'Ah the past is dark behind us
> Strewn with wrecks and stained with blood;
> But before us gleams the vision
> Of the coming brotherhood.'

If we can grasp the political initiative I believe the next general election could see the end of the old politics and the beginning of the new. I foresee a Liberal vote so massive and the number of Liberal MPs so great that we shall hold the initiative in the new Parliament. No government will be formed without us. I know that many unhappy MPs in the other parties will be ready to ally themselves with us once that moment comes.

Liberals and their progressive allies would come together to form what the country has needed for so long. A Liberal-led government, a government of partnership and reconciliation, one which will judge greatness not in the outmoded terms of imperial grandeur, the pursuit of selfish and superficial wealth, but in terms of the excellence of our education, the quality of our compassion, the health of our country, the harmony of our industrial life, and above all the humanity of our society.

By the next election we must give our people the chance they dearly want, the chance to elect a great government of national reform.

1981

Launching the Alliance.

Chapter Six

Fellow soldiers in a common warfare

Those contemplating the end of their political life in the Labour Party faced an awesome choice. Conflicting emotions of loyalty and friendship; frustration and anger; hope and despair had all crowded in. Some had resolved the intense personal conflict by slipping away quietly, like David Marquand, who had resigned his safe seat at Ashfield some years earlier and headed for the European Commission. But for those who wished to remain active in British political life, there were really only two options.

The first was to join a different Party. Reg Prentice, drummed out of Newham North-West, had briefly passed for a quiet chat at the Liberal Whip's Office before heading rightwards for the safer bosom of the Conservative Party. He was later to be rewarded with a safe seat at Daventry and, briefly, Ministerial office. But the more obvious haven for defecting Labour MPs was the Liberal Party, where they could expect a much greater coincidence of policy and attitudes. Christopher Mayhew, the Labour MP for Woolwich East and a former Defence Minister, had chosen that course in July 1974 and had become a stalwart figure in the Liberal Party as the candidate for Bath and, later, as a member of the House of Lords.

But there were hesitations. A number of those contemplating the break had held Ministerial office, a few at very senior level. They had been used to decades of influence and activity at the very centre of British politics. By contrast, the Liberal Party appeared peripheral and inconsequential, too much a Party of cranky amateurs.

The only other option — to create a new Party altogether — was no less perilous. That, too, had been tried before. Desmond Donnelly, in dispute with his Party at Pembroke, had briefly announced the formation of the Democratic Party, before disappearing in oblivion at the 1970 election.

Eddie Milne, the Labour MP for Blyth, and driven to dissent only because of his concern with corruption in the North-East of England, held out against the machine for a short while. But his Independent Labour Party never looked like being more than local and temporary.

More substantial in every way had been the actions of Dick Taverne, a talented former junior Treasury Minister. Hounded for holding to what had been respectable Labour views on Europe, and against unilateral disarmament, he had rounded on his increasingly left-wing constituency Labour Party and had forced a by-election at Lincoln. In an exciting and colourful campaign, he romped home with a majority of over 13,000. The Democratic Labour Party was hurriedly born and captured control of Lincoln City Council. In his personal testament "The Future of the Left", Dick Taverne chronicled the whole affair and set out the case for political realignment. It was a courageous step into the unknown and one which most pointed the way for the SDP seven years later.

Candidates were selected for half a dozen seats, including against Tony Benn in Bristol, but at the General Election of February 1974 only Taverne performed at all creditably, holding on to Lincoln with a reduced majority. By October that, too, had gone and the experiment was at an end; too localised, too much centred around the strength of a single personality, and too weak to withstand the crushing power of the two-party system.

Still, by the winter of 1980, most of the Labour rebels had reason to believe that with enough strength in numbers and with leaders, like Roy Jenkins, David Owen, Shirley Williams and Bill Rodgers, capable of capturing the public imagination, a new Party could be viable.

One of those from whom the rebels received encouragement was David Steel. A few had suggested joining the Liberal Party. Several more, including Roy Jenkins, saw it as one of the options. But the

Liberal Leader knew that there were others — perhaps the majority — who would not be able to bring themselves to take that step, for a variety of reasons. The whole impact of the breakout, he thought, would be gravely hampered.

One thing on which Steel was clear, and which had been recognised in a secret paper circulated by Tom Ellis, the MP for Wrexham, was that it would be madness to form a Fourth Party, to compete against the Third Party, in an overwhelmingly hostile Two-Party environment. That would be suicidal. An accommodation between the two — and, Steel insisted, an alliance of principle as well as an electoral arrangement — was an absolute necessity.

By the time of the Special Labour Conference at Wembley, in January 1981, the die was cast. David Owen made a brave but fruitless speech against the decision to change the system of electing the Labour Leader from a vote of the Parliamentary Labour Party to that of an electoral college, with the Trade Unions holding the dominant part.

A week later the Gang of Four issued the Limehouse Declaration. The calamitous outcome of the Labour Party Wembley conference, they said:

> "demands a new start in British politics.
> Our intention is to rally all those who are committed to the values, principles and policies of Social Democracy. We seek to reverse Britain's economic decline. We want to create an open, classless and more equal society, one which rejects ugly prejudices based upon sex, race or religion . . .
> We recognise that for those people who have given much of their lives to the Labour Party, the choice that lies ahead will be deeply painful. But we believe that the need for a realignment of British politics must now be faced."

A Council for Social Democracy was formed, with its feet still ostensibly in the Labour Party, but increasingly breathing the heady air of freedom. By the beginning of March, twelve Labour MPs had resigned the Labour Whip, including David Owen, and on the 26 March 1981, the Social Democratic Party was born, its ranks swollen by a steady stream of Labour defectors and the addition of a solitary Tory, Christopher Brocklebank-Fowler, the MP for Norfolk North-West.

The opinion polls immediately registered extraordinary levels of support for the new Party, more so when combined in alliance with the Liberal Party. The whole really did seem greater than the sum of the two parts. The Alliance had to be forged — and quickly — though it had to be a meeting of minds and hearts, rather than simply a product of electoral expediency.

In June 1981, David Steel and Shirley Williams together launched the first joint policy statement of the two Parties: "A Fresh Start for Britain". The document was short and to the point, setting out areas of policy agreement over proportional representation and parliamentary reform, support for NATO and for the EEC, devolution, a Freedom of Information Act, industrial partnership and an end to the adversarial system of Government.

The first big test for the new Alliance came in July 1981 at Warrington, a safe Labour seat. The Liberal candidate withdrew in favour of Roy Jenkins who bravely took up the challenge declined, with some hesitation, by Shirley Williams. Despite the mockery of the Press, who confidently expected Jenkins to be quite unsuitable for contesting a seat in Labour's industrial heartland, the SDP came astonishingly close to triumph. Although defeated by 1,759 votes, Roy Jenkins declared it "by far the greatest victory in which I have participated".

More than anything else, the Warrington by-election campaign helped allay Liberal fears and suspicions and paved the way for the crucial Assembly vote in September.

It was particularly poignant that this further consummation in the cause of political realignment should take place at the North Wales seaside resort of Llandudno, where David Steel had made his first controversial speech as Leader five years before. The Alliance with the SDP was endorsed by an overwhelming vote of 1,500 in favour, with only 112 in opposition. The result, which had not been in doubt after a memorable 'fringe' meeting at the start of the Assembly, had set the mood for the week. After electric speeches from Roy Jenkins, David Steel, Shirley Williams and an inspired Jo Grimond, the feeling had been intense.

By the end of the week, it was left to David Steel to point the Party to the future, in the knowledge that while the opportunity open to the new Alliance, as fellow soldiers in a common warfare, could be immense, the dangers of disunity and disagreement could also jeopardise everything.

> When we left Blackpool a year ago, it was in a mood of optimism and expectation. The year that has passed has fully justified that mood. The opinion polls during this year have been giving the Liberal Party our highest ratings since 1973; if you take poll ratings for the Liberal-Social

Democrat Alliance these are far higher than those ever achieved by our Party alone since opinion polls were invented.

And this year, we have enjoyed the greatest electoral advance of the Liberal Party since 1929 with the election of 400 councillors in every part of Britain and more victories every week. I congratulate all those who have contributed to that solid achievement.

This has been an outstandingly good Assembly. Don't take my word for it, take George Gale in yesterday's *Daily Express:* "this is not only the best Liberal Party Assembly I have ever attended; it is the best Liberal Party I have encountered."

Mind you we'll never convince some of the press. Our optimism in looking forward to 1981 was not universally shared. I give you this moving tale from "Crossbencher" of the *Sunday Express:*

"Which politician peers into the future with most trepidation on this last Sunday of 1980? Not Mrs Margaret Thatcher. She is sure her policies will start to bear fruit in the coming year.
"Certainly not Mr Michael Foot. He is convinced he is set firm to be the next occupant of Number 10.
"Whose heart, then, is a flutter with alarm? I give you the Liberal Leader, Mr David Steel.
"Nothing, but nothing, is going Mr Steel's way. If ever there was a time, he knows, when the Liberals should be riding high, that time is now.
"Yet gloomily he espies a steady slump, and that decline, he fears, could go from bad to catastrophic in 1981."

If the Liberal advance of 1981 can be described as catastrophic I hope Crossbencher will soon be telling us 1982 will be one long unmitigated disaster.

It is five years since we were last here in Llandudno when I made my first speech to you as the Party's new leader. What an extraordinary five years it has been for all of us. I've been looking back to what I said then.

"We are in being as a political party to form a government so as to introduce the policies for which we stand . . . I do not expect to lead just a nice debating society . . . we shall probably have — at least temporarily — to share power with somebody else to bring about the changes we seek . . . I want the Liberals to be an altogether tougher and more determined force. I want us to be a crusading and campaigning movement, not an academic think tank nor occasional safety-valve in the political system . . . the road I intend to travel may be a bumpy one, and I recognise the risk that in the course of it we may lose some of the passengers, but I don't mind so long as we arrive at the end of it reasonably intact and ready to achieve our goals."

The road over the last few years has certainly been a bumpy one. Life for the passengers has at times been very uncomfortable and worrying but we've lost surprisingly few. Actually, life in the driving seat hasn't been all that smooth either. But you may have noticed we've picked up some hitch hikers.

Here again in Llandudno in 1981 we can see our Party more tested, more organised, more mature and more prepared for the final electoral breakthrough.

It is as well for our country that the Liberal Party is so ready. For just look at the state of the nation in 1981. We have the highest unemployment figures since the 1930s. We have an annual inflation rate which in spite of two years' so called priority fight against it is nearly 12% and now rising again. This month's tax and prices index was announced this morning at 15%. We have a housebuilding rate which has sunk to its lowest level since 1948. In fact there are now more homeless people than when the Shelter campaign started. We have a commitment to the escalating costs of Trident which will make our expenditure on Concorde look like pocket-money for Dinky toys. We have riots in our city streets with many young people, both black and white, feeling angry and shut out. The nation's tax burden has increased in the last two years, and yet our educational system is falling apart from the cuts in government expenditure. This government is so penny pinching that it has even been prepared to cut back the overseas services of the BBC — in which we have justly taken world-wide pride for decades.

It is a grim picture which Britain presents to the rest of the world in this last quarter of the twentieth century — tired, shoddy and mean spirited — a picture made all the uglier because neither the government nor the official opposition hold out any prospect that they can solve our problems.

Cabinet reshuffles cannot disguise the fact that this Tory government has proved a total failure.

Our Prime Minister is a woman who has first turned her back on those who elected her and then had the nerve to claim that the people are behind her. Well, she still had seven per cent of them behind her at Warrington.

Margaret Thatcher has portrayed herself as the nation's nurse administering nasty but necessary medicine in the belief that whatever short term pain we may suffer, in the long run it will do us good. I am surprised that as a qualified chemist she seems to have forgotten the warning on every bottle: "Caution, it is dangerous to exceed the stated dose."

When I listen to her I am reminded of Somerset Maugham's description of her predecessor Neville Chamberlain as "sincere no doubt and honest, but muddled with self-conceit who put his party before his country, and by his ineptitude and stubbornness brought it to the verge of ruin."

As for the Labour opposition, who should be riding high in the effort to turn out this government, they claim to be the Party of brotherhood, but they seem to have taken their interpretation of it from the earliest biblical example — Cain and Abel.

It doesn't really matter whether Denis Healey or Tony Benn is the bloodstained victor. Neither the bankrupt right nor the hard left of the Labour Party have anything to offer this country any more. Their slide downhill has gone too far. It is irretrievable and irrecoverable. The Party's over.

Michael Foot said the other day that if his Party didn't come to its senses they would generate a decade of Thatcher government. But he's wrong, because at the next election we intend to provide the British electorate with a wider choice than that between the frying pan and the fire.

It was inevitable that this 1981 Liberal Assembly should be dominated both by public debate and private discussion of our Alliance.

This town used to be part of Lloyd George's constituency. Two years before the great Liberal landslide of 1906, the years which introduced the People's Budget, the old age pension, unemployment benefit, and the curbing of the powers of the hereditary Lords over the elected Commons, he gave advice which seems just as appropriate today two years or so before the next election.

"We have arrived at one of the most important stages in the history of the Liberal Party. I believe the future of this country largely depends upon the foresight, conviction, courage and devotion to principle of the Liberal Party during the coming years."

Our debates have carried conviction, courage, principle and foresight in full measure in these last few days. The task of putting together our Alliance on the ground throughout the country is not going to be an easy one. We must secure a reasonable balance in our deployment of forces in every area. It will be immensely complicated. It will call for a high degree of vision, of trust and of forbearance both by our Party and by the SDP.

It will require trust *between* our two Parties. The members of the SDP who have been here this week have been greatly impressed in their first close contact with the Liberal Party. They have also enjoyed the warmth of their welcome, and we were right to treat them kindly since they've come from a broken home — the Labour Party.

I hope they won't mind if I give them one piece of advice: as the ship of the Labour Party sinks, be careful and be discriminating about who you let clamber on board ours. Ours is a ship on a voyage of adventure. Don't let it become a lifeboat for those whose only real interest is saving their Parliamentary or Council skins.

It will also require trust *within* our Party. I want to thank you for the very considerable trust you have shown me in what I realise must at times have been a tortuous and anxious period. Now it is my turn to trust you as you proceed to give effect to our Alliance throughout the country. And I do trust you to make a success of it.

Our political situation is unique. Political parties normally seek to persuade the public to follow them. For the last few months the voice of the public as registered in the polls has been desperately pleading with our two political parties. Their message has been: "get together for *our* sakes."

They know our country is at a low ebb. The years of mismanagement have destroyed confidence. Broken promises have bred cynicism. The taste of failure is sour and bitter. We don't simply face an economic slump in Britain. What we have to deal with is more complex, a crisis of a whole society which has lost its way and turned in upon itself.

The challenge is daunting. It is a challenge to new leadership and new imagination. Four great tasks await the next government:

industrial reconstruction — to get the factories, offices and workshops humming with activity again;

social reconciliation — to bring together a people divided against each other and restore a sense of the common weal amongst all our peoples;

a new constitutional settlement — which makes democratic and open self-government its guiding principle;

an international role — which restores our influence abroad and makes us a force for peace and prosperity in the world.

These are the four cornerstones of the great reforming government I expect us to form with our Social Democratic allies.

Yes, government. You remember that truly remarkable speech on Tuesday by Jo Grimond. We felt the movement in the hall. But don't you feel the movement in the country? This Assembly has seen the Liberal Party discard its role of eternal opposition and face up to the realities of power. It is an awesome responsibility. Instead of criticising we must contribute. Instead of shouting on the sidelines, we must take over the game.

For I tell you this. When our Alliance government takes office, it will represent the last, best hope for the British people. Our fellow-citizens don't want another set of broken promises — followed by the usual search for scapegoats. They have seen enough of that from the Tory and Labour Parties. They want honesty, commitment and imagination. Our Alliance can only succeed if it calls upon the greatest under-used resource of all, the people themselves.

Our plan for recovery must depend upon creating a common purpose in which everyone has a part to play. That in turn depends upon us defining clearly what it is we are trying to achieve — and enlisting the help of every man and woman in these islands in our shared hope for the future.

I turn first then to industrial reconstruction, for without that many of our other plans for Britain will remain but pieces of paper.

First an Alliance government will end the damaging nationalisation versus privatisation see-saw so beloved by the Labour and Tory Parties. Our task will be to create conditions of maximum efficiency and morale in the public sector and maximum profit in the private sector, and to see each as complementary, not rival to the other. The remorseless trend towards unsuccessful merger, whether in the private or public sector, must be reversed. Smaller units can be more human, more imaginative and more profitable. The axiom that bigger is automatically better will find no place in the new government's industrial policy.

Indeed secondly we must encourage the innovation of small businesses and co-operatives with positive fiscal discrimination in their favour. You remember the Tories' pledge to help small businesses? Experience has shown that the only sure way to run a small business today in Tory Britain is to start with a large one.

Thirdly, in public spending we could reduce the waste of unemployment by selective forward investment on such essential items as our railways and telephone system and especially on home improvements which would help the building industry and increase our housing stock. I have in mind in particular the need to expand our programme of insulating buildings in the interests of saving energy.

Far from saving energy, this government is determined to waste it. Already £500 million of North Sea gas has been burned off into the atmosphere. Another £25,000 million-worth is there to be exploited; and yet Mrs. Thatcher has sacrificed the gas-gathering pipeline on the altar of the Public Sector Borrowing Requirement. That pipeline would have meant 3,000 jobs in British Steel, as well as assuring long-term supplies to British Gas and future revenue to the British government. What economic madness has gripped the Treasury, that it uses the revenues of North Sea oil to pay people *not* to work, but is incapable of devising a scheme which would not only put many of those people into work but would bring a profitable return to the Exchequer from one of the richest resources this country has ever possessed? This sheer waste of human and natural resources is downright immoral.

It's the same story with the Severn barrage, which Liberals have long advocated. It was judged both feasible and economic in a study sponsored by the Department of Energy and published in July — which the government launched with a fanfare of one penny whistle. In contrast, Mrs. Thatcher's nuclear obsessions continue to escalate in price, and the new Pressurised Water Reactor is sanctioned, while fears about safety remain unanswered.

But the fourth and greatest economic challenge for the Alliance government will be to change not just policies, but attitudes which have thwarted Britain's industrial progress. Remember the extraordinary levels of high productivity reached during the three day week? Why do we assume that such successful communal effort is only possible in times of national adversity be it war or power cuts? Labour and Tory governments have proved institutionally incapable of breaking down the class barriers which bedevil our country more than any other.

"If you live in what is probably the most advanced political democracy in the world, where individual freedom of thought and action is pursued and respected, how can you expect people to behave differently within the factory

fence and office location? How can you expect that people will do things because you tell them to and not because they understand why?"

These are not my words, but those of Sir Ray Pennock, President of the CBI, who is doing so much to try to change outdated attitudes there. But the next government must give a lead in creating a united and fulfilled commercial life in our country — and in this our proposed legislation for profit sharing and industrial partnership has a major part to play. You remember the tax incentive scheme for employee shareholding we got through in 1978 in the Lib-Lab Pact? Well the figures for 1980/81 show that we've at least made a dent in the institutions' domination of the stock market. We have increased by 25% the number of individual adults who own shares in Britain.

Much more could be done to create harmony and therefore efficiency and therefore jobs. So, fifthly, I believe that one of our most important tasks in the next government will be not only to spread the sharing of increased wealth, but to relate our traditional policies of co-partnership to the difficult but crucial question of a prices and incomes policy.

There is no need for us to get bogged down in a dispute between the merits of statutory versus voluntary policy. Clearly we need to secure the widest national consent for it, but its operation must be flexible, not rigid, and adaptable to the different circumstances of different enterprises. If, for example, we recommend a policy involving tax incentives for organisations which settle within agreed guidelines, that is certainly both voluntary and flexible in character but would require statutory authority to operate.

The importance of incomes policy in controlling inflation was the theme of a long study this summer by the American liberal economist J.K. Galbraith in which he concluded: "The purpose of an incomes and prices policy is to reduce the reliance on fiscal and monetary policy. Both of these work against inflation, but only as they create idle capacity and unemployment. It is one of Britain's great, useful and painful contributions to economic understanding that it has shown that this is not an economist's theory; it is a matter of practical experience."

The country is tired of being the unfortunate experimental model for Mrs. Thatcher's economic advisers.

The Tories said they could do without an incomes policy. Now they've got a sort of policy, cobbled together like its predecessors; 4% for the public sector, fear of unemployment for the rest.

We don't pretend that incomes policy is an ideal instrument of economic management. It is not. It involves difficult and frustrating negotiation. Its justification is not that it is agreeable. It is that incomes policy is far superior to unemployment and recession.

Next I want to turn to the question of social reconciliation. There can be no reconciliation without a determined search for social justice.

The other day Mr. John Alderson, the Chief Constable of Devon and

Cornwall, and incidentally formerly deputy commissioner of the Metropolitan Police, in a very courageous and forthright statement said:

"People who are poor and have a chip on their shoulders against society are inclined to say: 'I am getting nothing out of life so I am going to be angry'.
"If society then says: 'Okay, you can get as angry as you like, but I have a well-paid fat-cat police force and if you get angry I shall just clobber you,' then we are making a big mistake.
"One thing is certain — it is no answer to resort to brute force to try to control people."

Remember the havoc and terror caused by the police raids on Railton Road, Brixton, on 15th July, attacks which moved Lord Scarman to say the damage had caused him "an immense amount of distress and that the question of compensation was no substitute".

Remember that these attacks took place at 3 o'clock in the morning, a time normally associated with totalitarian regimes and police states — the knock on the door in the night. The new Bishop of Southwark, whose diocese includes Brixton, said in the House of Lords: "The way in which policing has been carried out in Brixton has been a major factor in the deterioration of the situation there."

We must in the light of all this demand that police actions be made open to an independent complaints body, the present system having proved itself to be wholly and woefully inadequate.

That's fair to the public and fair to the police. They have had a lot to put up with too.

Much injury to our police in riots in London, Liverpool and Manchester was caused by outside agitators. I have no doubt that there are people whose main object is to exploit the grievances by fomenting unrest; but they could only have been successful because existing conditions were favourable for them. Mosquitoes can only breed if the water itself is already swampy and stagnant.

I am against day to day police administration being interfered with by outsiders as some are advocating, but I do believe it is the task of the government in an elected parliament to lay down the broad policy for our policing — to choose between competing approaches — and I believe we should utterly reject the view of the secretary of the Police Federation that we should "forget about the cosy image of Dixon of Dock Green". The whole point of Dixon was that he knew and lived among the people he was policing, but you cannot resurrect Dixon of Dock Green if you have demolished Dock Green police station and retreated to centralised office blocks with motorised patrols.

If community policing works in the city of Plymouth it can work elsewhere. In any case community policing *is* already practised successfully elsewhere — I've seen it in my own constituency, here in

North Wales and even in a part of Liverpool. But I'd like to see it everywhere. Liberals say, put the policeman back into the community, not just as a law enforcement officer, but as a social leader working with the local people.

But it isn't just policing or unemployment which we should blame for these disturbances. It's the attitude of successive governments, indeed in the end it's our own attitudes as well. Governments have propounded the myth that strict immigration laws are necessary for good race relations, whereas this is the exact reverse of the truth. Ever since the dishonourable Act of 1968, and the more squalid one of 1971 which gave the police the vast powers they now so wrongly have with regard to immigration matters, legislation has become steadily harsher, and very naturally community relations have equally steadily deteriorated. You cannot dehumanise a whole section of society by taking away their rights, dividing their families, subjecting them to police and bureaucratic interference and harassment, and then pretend as the Tories do — that great Party of the family — that this is all done in the interests of good race relations.

The new Nationality Bill has been brought in by this government very largely to satisfy the ugly side of the Tory Party and the nation — a side to which the Prime Minister herself has made a more than generous contribution.

Yet when the clergy, who, being on the spot, are as good judges of the situation as any, voice their criticisms, they are immediately attacked by Tory MPs and the Tory press as "trendy lefties" and told to go back to their task of preaching the Gospel. I noticed that during the debate on the Nationality Bill in the House of Commons, Tory racialism and Tory vituperation of the churches — to the great credit of the church — went hand in hand.

Immigration itself is no longer the central issue. The era of massive immigration into Britain has clearly ended. An increasingly large proportion of the black and brown population of this country are native British, born and bred. We *cannot* allow them to grow up as second-class citizens. We need more positive action, in education, in employment, to ensure that they can enjoy the same range of rights and opportunities that the rest of us take for granted. A programme for citizen equality must begin with the rejuvenation of our inner cities, where so many of our more recent immigrant families still live; but must extend well beyond, to encompass recruitment and promotions within the Government Service, and encouragement for affirmative action in the private sector.

The fight against racialism is one of the most important concerns of my political life, and I could not be a member of any Alliance that did not have as one of its major commitments not just the removal of present racist legislation, but a firm and unequivocal determination to establish racial *justice*, without which racial *harmony* is impossible.

The third plank in the new government's platform will be constitutional reform.

The British constitution was once a fertile source of inspiration for every nation which believed in democratic government and the rule of law. It stood for the will of the majority and the protection of minorities. That is so no longer. The source has dried up and we are left with barren institutions, ineffective and susceptible to take-over by arrogant minorities who want to impose their will on the rest of us.

We need a new constitutional settlement — and I must tell you what an enormous cause of satisfaction it has been to me this year that our Social Democratic allies have come to share the Liberal prescription: the first step must be a genuinely democratic proportional representation system of voting. But we do not stop there. We need devolution of power to the regions and nations of Britain; an end to official secrecy; and far greater protection of the rights of the individual. We have to make real democracy work so well that the pretensions of the Labour Left for whom democracy begins and ends with party membership are exposed for the power-hungry sham they are.

A new constitutional settlement means freedom and democracy, but it also means better government, open, participative, and in touch with the people it represents.

One of the aims of our constitutional settlement must be the reduction of government, not its increase — one of the fatal flaws in Labour's devolution schemes. This means re-creating *local* government which the Tories seem hell bent on destroying first by their changes of 1973 and now by financial strangulation. We must be ready to reduce bureaucracy by streamlining local government including the abolition of the metropolitan counties in England, the counties in Wales and creating single tiers out of the regions and districts in Scotland.

Nor can we leave Northern Ireland in its acrimonious stalemate. We should take further some of the excellent ideas in our debate this week. Like the new Irish premier Garrett FitzGerald we want to bring our islands closer together using the opportunities provided by our common membership of the European Community.

This brings me to the fourth objective of the Alliance government, to restore our international influence.

The European Community is wallowing in arguments about butter, fish and wine. My good friend and Liberal colleague, Hans Dietrich Genscher, the Foreign Minister of Germany, has put forward some imaginative proposals for reform. President Mitterand's new administration, too, is formulating its ideas for a "relaunching" of the European ideal. Yet this Tory government can only see the small change of Europe, not the wider vision. Britain ought to be a major influence on the development of Europe — and a united Europe should be a major influence for peace and security in our world. I applaud the European initiatives on the Middle-

East and on Afghanistan, but we should be doing far more as a Community to implement some of the major economic recommendations of the Brandt report.

The Tories' attitude to the grim statistics of world poverty is an international disgrace. They are like the first-class passengers in the bow of a liner saying "we're all right — it is your end of the boat that is sinking". We can make no such divisions in our world. The decision to force up overseas student fees was an act of barbarism; in many parts of the world this year I found it one of the most short sighted and damaging from the point of view of Britain's *own* long term economic and political interests.

We have also failed to give united impetus in Europe to a new disarmament initiative. European Liberal leaders have made it clear that we must push the USA and the USSR towards nuclear disengagement.

Of course as we saw yesterday, Liberals have genuine and deeply felt differences on *how* we can best get disarmament. But if the Soviet Union can be persuaded to withdraw her SS 20's, cruise missiles will not be required in Europe. That should be our objective over the next few years.

Unfortunately our Prime Minister too often gives positive tuition to President Reagan in cold war rhetoric. It is time we got to grips with President Brezhnev to get him to translate his fine sounding speeches into positive actions to reduce the stockpile of terror in the world. For as Einstein once said "if the third world war is fought with nuclear weapons the fourth will be fought with bows and arrows."

Our commitment to collective western security in the defence of freedom must be maintained. The threat to Poland should remind us of the need for eternal vigilance. And our dedication to liberty means that we must oppose the indifference to human rights which the Reagan administration is showing by its support for such unsavoury regimes as those in South Africa and El Salvador.

In selecting these four subjects for my address this year I am not of course attempting to detail all of Liberal policies. I welcome the publication of our mid-term programme which does that far more adequately. What is important in our Alliance is that we are agreed on the main priorities for a new radical government while each Party is free to develop its own detailed policies.

Liberalism is not just the creed of a political party. It is the expression of a profoundly moral view of human nature and its possibilities. For too long the Liberal values of tolerance, mutual respect and co-operation have been on the defensive against the zealots of right and left. Liberals themselves have sometimes been defensive, with the attitudes and concerns of a persecuted minority. There has even been a tendency to say: keep Liberalism out of politics.

But that time is over. The relevance of Liberalism, which has sometimes been drowned out by the clamour of the extremists, is sharp and clear today.

It is time to assert our Liberalism proudly — and nowhere more so than in this new Alliance. We must provide the heart and soul of the Alliance, proud of being Liberals and glad to work with those who have come to agree with us.

The great debate we have had this week about our future has not just been of importance to the Party, it has been of supreme importance to the country. There are those who say that the Liberals and Social Democrats are like two teams of people who find themselves on the summit of the same mountain having got there from different starting places and by different routes. I am not sure that that analogy is entirely correct. Of course we have come by different routes, but I am not certain that the starting place wasn't in fact the same.

Remember that the social democrats who worked within the Labour Party for years based their creation of the welfare state and the planned economy on the work of great Liberals like Beveridge and Keynes. Somewhere after we left our common starting point they lost their way. The Labour Party took the wrong path, to state socialism, bureaucracy, centralised controls and mandate by caucus — that perversion of democracy. But the social democrats have now found their way to rejoin us.

Our Liberalism must be tolerant of those going through the travail of re-examining political allegiances often held since childhood.

I was given a few weeks ago a set of leather bound speeches of my great predecessor, William Ewart Gladstone. On his way to the historic Midlothian campaign he stopped at Hawick in my constituency and there delivered a short speech which with only a couple of words changed has an uncanny application to our Party today:

"We are comrades in a common undertaking; we are fellow soldiers in a common warfare; we have a very serious labour to perform. The people of this country, and you among them in your place, have to consider what is the system upon which we ought to be governed. We should endeavour to bring about a great and fundamental change in regard to those dangerous novelties which have of late been introduced into the policy of this country, which have disturbed the world at large, and which have certainly aggravated the distress of the nation at home. I believe that in our efforts to return to the sound and just Liberal principles that have commonly distinguished in our time British administration we have in our charge a cause which is the cause of peace, which is the cause of justice, which is the cause of liberty, which is the cause of honour, and which, in the hands of the people of this country by the blessing of God will not fail."

Our Alliance has caught people's imaginations. You can see it in opinion polls and in the latest local by-election victories — six more yesterday.

Warrington showed it and Croydon will show it again. The voters are responding to the sight of politicians of different tradition but similar persuasion getting together and sinking differences for the common good.

They respect an alliance of principle because they can see that an Alliance is the way forward: the Alliance for Britain, where people can be brought together.

An alliance between management and labour, a real partnership to restore pride in our work and confidence in our industry. An alliance between young and old, in which the young are given the chance they need and the old the respect they deserve. An alliance in the economy, between a private sector dedicated to productivity and a public sector committed to service and efficiency. An alliance between black people and white people, so that *all* the communities of Britain can make a contribution to the solution of our problems. In short, an Alliance which pulls our country together — instead of the old Parties which have torn it apart.

An Alliance which discards the envy and pettiness of the past, which stands for all the people and our hope for the future. This has been the dream that has sustained the Liberal Party for so many long weary years. Now at last we have the reality in our grasp. We must have the nerve and courage not to let it slip.

I have the good fortune to be the first Liberal Leader for over half a century who is able to say to you at the end of our annual Assembly: go back to your constituencies and prepare for government.

1982

Campaigning for Roy Jenkins at Hillhead.

Chapter Seven

Back to the constituencies

After the euphoria of Llandudno, the new Alliance faced an early test of its resolve and unity. A vacancy had arisen in the south London Parliamentary seat of Croydon North-West. The Liberals already had a candidate in place, who had fought several preceding elections, although not with a great deal of success.

The SDP on the other hand, with some encouragement from David Steel, saw the by-election as an ideal opportunity for Shirley Williams to seek a dramatic return to Parliament. The seat was in any case a Conservative-Labour marginal, the kind of territory where the Liberals had rarely performed well in the past. In the circumstances, some felt that only a candidate with the personality and national reputation of Mrs. Williams would be equal to the daunting electoral task.

Bill Pitt, the prospective Liberal candidate, not unnaturally disagreed, and insisted on standing his ground. The Liberal candidate at Warrington, after all, had withdrawn in favour of Roy Jenkins and, with a queue of leading SDP personalities itching for the chance of fighting a by-election, some Liberal activists feared that to defer once more might create a habit.

The whole controversy had the effect of giving Bill Pitt 'folk hero' status within the Liberal Party, 'local hero' in Croydon, and more generally giving him precisely that degree of national media exposure which his critics had suggested he was incapable of generating.

The matter was not pressed, and the leadership swung behind Mr Pitt's campaign with gusto. On 22 October, all received their reward. The Liberals had achieved a famous victory, taking 13,800 votes, more than 3,000 votes clear of the Conservatives and almost 5,000 ahead of the Labour candidate, who finished in third place. The Alliance had won its first Parliamentary seat; the Liberals their first ever Tory-Labour marginal in modern times; and the name of William Pitt was once more inscribed on the roll of Parliamentary members.

But Shirley Williams was soon to have her chance. The comfortable Merseyside constituency of Crosby, with a huge Tory majority of over 18,000, had become vacant. This time there were no arguments about who should be the Alliance candidate, with both Liberal and SDP members thin on the ground.

The task was monumental — and the redoubtable Shirley Williams equal to the task. In a staggering turnabout of votes, she swept to victory with 28,118 votes, against the Tory candidate's 22,829. The SDP, with their Liberal partners, had captured their first Parliamentary seat in an election, and had done so in what had been one of the safest Conservative seats in the country. Labour lost their deposit.

The victory at Crosby represented the frothy pinnacle and although the Alliance made solid local by-election gains — winning one seat for every two contested in the last half of 1981 — nothing quite matched the highwater mark of Crosby.

Yet there were victories to come, most notably — and most deservedly — at Glasgow Hillhead, where the courageous Roy Jenkins, once more facing a degree of media hostility, took the seat in a closely fought contest. His majority over the Conservatives, of just over 2,000, was small, and Labour were less than 3,000 behind. Nonetheless, it was a seat he was to hold from Labour at the General Election.

Yet, three days after Glasgow Hillhead voted, the British political mood was to undergo a sea-change — with the Alliance (which six months earlier had actually registered 50% support in the opinion polls) finding itself on the ebb tide.

The cause was the Argentinian invasion of the Falkland Islands, and the despatch of a large British naval task force to liberate the 1,800 islanders and restore by military valour what had been lost through political incompetence.

Not unnaturally, with the lives of British servicemen and national pride at stake, the people of Britain rallied to their Government in a wave of patriotic fervour. Try as they might, the Labour Party and the Alliance struggled to disentangle the electorate's strong feelings of national solidarity — which were widely shared — from a pavlovian wish to vote for the Conservative Government whenever the opportunity arose. But it was to no avail, and the 'Falklands factor' became a new phenomenon in British politics. At the beginning of 1982, Mrs Thatcher had the unique distinction of being Britain's least popular national leader on record, with Tory support in the opinion polls below 30%. By the end of the Falklands campaign, with the Union Jack once more flying above Port Stanley, the Conservatives had surged to an unassailable lead of 20% in the polls.

In the local elections in May 1982, the effects of this new development began to be apparent. Despite a highly respectable average vote of 28%, the Alliance made an overall gain of only ninety-seven councillors, with the more deeply entrenched Liberals winning five times as many seats as their less established SDP partners. And the Alliance was given an ominous warning of the vagaries of the electoral system. In Stockport, for example, the Alliance won only four seats for its vote of 36,380, while the Conservatives netted 11 seats with only 35,605 votes.

Further disappointments were to come. In June, after a discouraging result in the Beaconsfield by-election, the Alliance lost the seat of Mitcham and Morden, after the former Labour MP had nobly resigned his seat on joining the SDP in order to seek a fresh mandate from his electorate. This quixotic gesture was as disastrous electorally as it was unwelcome to the Alliance leadership. Nor did the by-election at Coatbridge, where the Alliance candidate came fourth, provide any cheer.

By the time Liberals gathered in September, in the salubrious surroundings of Bournemouth, David Steel knew the Alliance had to deal with its faltering electoral momentum. This was not solely due to Mrs Thatcher's triumph in the South Atlantic — although through the testing summer every feat of British arms pushed Tory support in the polls up a notch or two. There were also continued rumblings over the allocation of Parliamentary seats between the two parties. By and large, this carve-up of constituencies had been achieved without too much bloodletting and on the basis of fairly rough justice. But this unedifying public spectacle had taken its toll of support and done nothing to enhance the lustre of two distinct parties, working in perfect harmony.

There were certain constituencies where agreement had ostensibly been reached but where the decision was clearly wrong — with the resulting damage to the local parties and their political credibility having a fatal effect on the Alliance challenge in those areas. There also remained around thirty constituencies where the dispute between the two sides remained unresolved. While these were eventually whittled down to a handful by the time of the General Election, they had a debilitating effect both on the energies of the leadership and the local activists concerned, and on the national image of the Alliance.

A further source of friction had arisen over the question of the Alliance Leader. For a while, after the birth of the SDP, politicians, journalists and the public were prepared to accept that each Party had its own leader and that the Alliance was under the direction of a limited partnership, rather than a sole proprietor.

But as the General Election approached, the media's desire to view the contest in quasi-presidential terms became irresistible. It was not until the end of the year that the rather unconvincing and pompous compromise — of two Leaders, but with Roy Jenkins as "Prime Minister-designate" and David Steel as chairman of the election campaign — came into the public domain. But the tensions caused by the controversy were ever-present, especially among Liberals who feared that their popular leader was once again selling himself short.

Above all, as David Steel came onto the platform of the Pavilion Theatre to deliver his Seventh Annual Assembly Speech, he knew that the Liberal Party, and the Alliance, had to be knocked into fighting shape for the election which was likely to be upon them in the next six months:

> Last year I asked you to go back to your constituencies and prepare for government. In the years since then, we have won Croydon and our allies have won Crosby and Hillhead with our full participation and support. In May we established a record win of 400 local council seats. We now have a solid base — our largest ever total of 1,800 Liberal Councillors elected to authorities throughout the land.
>
> But a great deal of our energy and concentration has been devoted during the year to the cumbersome, complicated and contentious task of allocating the constituencies between Liberal and SDP candidates to make our Alliance effective. It is worth stressing again that the vast majority of these 600 individual decisions were achieved amicably and democratically between our two parties at local level.
>
> In about thirty cases we had real difficulty, the only surprise is that there were so few. At the end we have had to push through agreements with some acute disappointments in both parties, but more of course in ours where already adopted candidates have been asked to withdraw.

I understand the pain which these decisions have caused, but they had to be faced sometime and I want to say something to those candidates and those associations who will not be fighting the next election: when I listened to the oustandingly generous speeches made by some of the candidates personally affected through the week, I was proud to be leader of your Party. The role which you will play in providing the campaigning lead for our local government effort next May and for our SDP allies in the next general election is central to the success of our endeavour and therefore crucial to a liberal future.

A liberal future is now the alternative for our country. We have heard a great deal about there being "no alternative" to the present policies. It is a proposition which defies commonsense. It is quite simply Conservative propaganda — and I want to nail it once and for all.

Look around you. Is there no alternative to the silent factories with their machinery sold for scrap? No alternative to the dole queues and wasted lives? No alternative to the decaying cities and the shabby streets? Is there no alternative to the frustration of the young and the abandonment of the old? Is no progress possible? Is no change necessary?

We will never accept this Tory counsel of despair. There must be a better way for Britain than selfishness, violence and decline, than greed among the ruins. Unused skills and resources can and must be matched-up with unfulfilled needs. We believe like Martin Luther King that "what self-centred men have torn down, other-centred men can build up". We must throw away the economic dogma of the monetarists and the marxists alike and start again to use our own minds and imagination.

As we do this *we* shall become the real opposition to the Tories. The Labour Party have forfeited all claims to be considered as an acceptable alternative government. We have to fill the vacuum left by the intellectual and political collapse of that once great party.

Mr Foot said Mr Peter Tatchell would never be accepted as the Labour candidate at Bermondsey. Now he is. The militant tendency are condemned by an official report, yet their members are Labour parliamentary candidates in Liverpool and Bradford.

Tony Benn this week made a direct appeal for those Liberals disillusioned with our Alliance marriage to run off with him, presumably to help put asunder the Labour Party. Well I have news for him; there is a world of difference between our commitment to the values of generous and open minded Liberalism where the individual comes first and his argument for a narrow socialism where the state is supreme. This is a free party. If he's watching let him see there are no concrete walls keeping people in as exist round some societies whose system he admires. People are free to go — are there any takers?

No, the truth is Tony you've created a bit of a problem for us. So many people are now leaving the Labour Party because of the behaviour of you and your friends that we can't pack them all in here and for the first time at our Assembly hundreds of delegates have to watch on television in our overflow hall next door.

The social democratic part of that once great coalition which made up the Labour Party has lost the struggle and abandoned ship. The ship is breaking up leaving the Hattersleys and Heffers fighting vainly for control of the wreckage as it drifts towards the Shore.

Let us leave them to their absorbing task. We have to pick up the baton of responsible opposition now, and of credible alternative government at the next election.

I want today to read you a few choice sentences from a little book that I have enjoyed re-reading over the summer. It is a work laced with wonder, fantasy, excitement and promise. It is called "The Conservative Manifesto, 1979". The foreword is written by their leader and promises that the rest of the pages "set out a broad framework for the recovery of our country".

Let us test their achievements against that promise. I begin by giving credit where credit is due. After three years of struggle, pain and sacrifice during which the rate of inflation went as high as 22% they have got it back to 1% less than they inherited. The Tories proudly claimed last week that they had got inflation in Britain back to the level of 1979.

But that's not all they've got back to the levels of previous years. Manufacturing output is now back to the level of 1967. Manufacturing investment back to 1963. And the level of unemployment is back to the level of 1933.

When the Tories talked of backing Britain no-one realised that what they meant was putting the entire country into reverse.

They blame the world recession. But unemployment in Britain in the last three years has become twice the level of the rest of the EEC. Britain went earlier and deeper into the recession than any of our competitors pushed by the policies of the British government.

The manifesto said:

"Our country's relative decline is not inevitable, we in the Conservative Party think we can reverse it." A lot of people believed them. But no longer. All round, from the CBI to the TUC, from the academic world, from individual industrialists and economists, comes criticism which the Government refuses to heed. Typical is the latest *Midland Bank Review:* "It is now becoming doubtful whether a significant recovery can be achieved without reflationary action in which the Government takes the lead."

But the lady is, she tells us, not for turning. She's not for listening either. Her admirers liken her to Queen Boadicea. I regard her as a kind of Queen Canute sitting on the beach ignoring all advice as the tide of disaster rises around her.

This Government has reduced profitability in British industry to an all-time record low, left its plant, capacity, research and investment in a more debilitated condition than anyone of this generation can remember. The so-called party of business has created more bankruptcies and liquidations than any government this century.

Far from building a "broad framework for recovery", they have laid waste the economy with a ferocity unparalleled since Attila the Hun. They chose to ignore all the warnings that their cures would be worse than the disease. They have left our industries so weak that if the much awaited up-turn comes we may become unable to respond, and be left as helpless spectators while our competitors mop up the business.

And the most damning indictment of all is that this Government has squandered our national assets of North Sea Oil on the huge cost of our ever-lengthening dole queues.

Unemployment cost us £15 billion last year. And that is only the financial cost. The human cost is appalling. We are breeding a young generation many of whom have no idea how to work because they've never had a chance to do any. There is an older generation of men and women in their fifties too, who face the bitter realisation that they've been thrown on to the unemployment scrap heap, possibly for ever.

Amid this desolation one group of people remains determinedly cheerful. The members of the Cabinet. Listen to what they've been saying:

Mrs Thatcher told us in her New Year message that 1982 "has all the signs of being a year of great opportunity". I pointed out at the time that she must have forgotten that her 1981 New Year message told us: "there is a real hope that a year from now things will be looking distinctly brighter".

Every member of the Cabinet has been at it consistently over all three years: November 1980, Geoffrey Howe: "the fall in output is bottoming out";

December 1980, John Nott: "I think we have reached the bottom of the recession";

January 1981, Nigel Lawson: "all the signs suggest that we have now more or less reached the bottom";

May 1981, Michael Heseltine: "there is tangible evidence that the worst is over";

June 1981, Margaret Thatcher: "the recession has just about reached the bottom";

October 1981, Geoffrey Howe: "there are some clear signs that the Government's economic policy is beginning to work . . . we have passed the end of the beginning";

January 1982, Norman Tebbit: "we are beginning to see signs of our policies working";

February 1982, Patrick Jenkin: "we are on the verge of an export-led boom".

Last month, Norman Tebbit, losing his sense of direction altogether in a television interview proclaimed: "we are somewhere near the plateau — near the top".

All this from his Cabinet colleagues so confused poor Sir Keith Joseph that his only contribution to this stream of bogus propaganda last year was: "we are in the bottoming out phase, or very closely approaching it".

The very last sentence of the Tory manifesto reads: "the years of make-believe and false optimism are over". What people have got to realise before it is too late is that make-believe and false optimism are the entire threadbare stock-in-trade of this administration.

The bogus promises covered almost every item of policy. Take education.

The manifesto said "we must restore to every child, regardless of background, the chance for progress as far as his or her abilities allow". Falling school roles provide a unique opportunity to raise the quality of education by reducing class sizes. Yet this Government has left more trained teachers paid to be idle than ever before.

As for higher education they said: "much of it in Britain has a world-wide reputation for its quality. We shall seek to ensure that this excellence is maintained." Try telling that to the thousands of students with good A levels unable to gain places in college or university in these last two years. Even more try telling it to the poorer Commonwealth countries who because of this Government's fee increases can no longer afford to send students here, but send them instead to America, Japan or even Russia. What crass short-sighted political and commercial folly.

On housing, tenants were told: "we must try to achieve a greater take-up in rent allowances for poorer tenants". Greater take-up? They've abolished them altogether and are about to introduce a so-called housing benefit which will leave two million lower income tenants 75p a week poorer.

On mortgages, they said: "mortgage rates have risen steeply . . . our plans will lower them". The average mortgage rate during their period of office has been consistently at least 2% higher than they inherited and has twice reached 15%.

On energy, they said: "we attach particular importance to measures to reduce fuel consumption by improving insulation". They've reduced fuel consumption all right, but by pushing up prices and shutting down factories. Their record on insulation is so bad that this summer the Commons Select Committee complained about "lack of political will at the heart of Government which smothers the efforts of the Department of Energy's conservation division."

In their manifesto, the Tories stated: "the most disturbing threat to our freedom and security is the growing disrespect for the rule of law". Never have there been so many muggings, break-ins and burglaries. Not even Buckingham Palace has proved safe. Throughout the past three years the crime wave has left an indelible mark on the lives of thousands of people.

Mrs Thatcher blandly asserted that this break-down of law and order has nothing to do with the scale of unemployment. She chose to ignore what Lord Scarman said in his report: "There is no doubt that unemployment is a major factor in the complex pattern of conditions which lies at the root of the disorders in Brixton and elsewhere".

The Conservatives have shouted order but have denied justice; sooner or later they must understand that without justice, the police will not be able to maintain that order without recourse to methods unacceptable in a free society. The Government deserves credit for improving pay and recruitment in the police; but law and order will improve only when policy changes.

This Assembly gave overwhelming support to a resolution committed to community policing demanding a responsible and responsive police force.

Let me say a word about responsibility. We all learnt with horror of the brutal attack by seventeen policemen on an innocent West Indian couple who were wrongfully arrested and beaten up in their own home. They suffered such severe injury that in court, Mr Justice Mars Jones was moved to describe the police behaviour as "monstrous, wicked and shameful"; the matter he said had been deliberately covered up for five years. During this time no action was taken to suspend any of the officers concerned.

We in Britain have reason to be grateful for the high standards of the police. But that high reputation suffers if wrongdoing within the police force is swept under the carpet. It is just no answer to say that there are good and bad in every walk of life — and that therefore one must expect bad policemen. The custodians of law and order are themselves possessed of great power, especially over ethnic minorities under our inhuman immigration acts. They must not be allowed to have their crimes covered up by obliging superiors. That is not law and order — that is legalised disorder. That is why we insisted on seeing the Home Secretary about the failure of Operation Countryman.

If as speculated the Government's programme in the coming session includes random stop and search powers for the police, we will vehemently oppose them, because they would compound the sins of the past.

And to our ethnic minorities I repeat my pledge of last year, that I will not be party to any government that does not have, as one of its priorities, a commitment to remove all our present racist legislation, so that they may live their lives in dignity and peace, in a civilised society to which they have already contributed so much.

Returning to the Tory manifesto, the tax and social security section declared: "we shall cut income tax at all levels and tackle the poverty trap". In fact more people are now caught in the income tax net. A low paid couple on £80 a week find themselves paying in tax and national insurance 42% more than when this Government came to power.

They said they would "bring more effective help to those in need"; — yet they have reduced unemployment benefit by 5%. And they have let child benefit drop in real value.

Of the National Health Service they said: "standards are falling; there is a crisis of morale". So what have they done to improve morale in the Service? They have threatened to abolish it. And meanwhile they have put Norman Fowler in charge of it. With the other Norman in charge of the unemployed you have the two boot boys of British politics kicking in the windows of the welfare state.

What has happened to the Conservative Party? What have they done with the one nation tradition of Rab Butler, Iain Macleod and Edward Boyle? How have the decent Tories allowed their party to be hi-jacked by the heavy squad? How long will they put up with the unacceptable face of Conservatism?

Whilst I realise that it does not do to be too fastidious in politics, I have to confess to a real sense of repugnance at the way the Prime Minister has tried to use the heroism of British servicemen in the Falkland Islands campaign to the greater glory of herself and her Party. As one Tory MP wrote candidly on Sunday: "The party is high on the Falklands factor, the gift of courage and skill of our servicemen, which has served to mask for a time the realities of politics."

But that is not enough for the Prime Minister. She has presided over a shambles of incompetence in her conduct of foreign policy and defence. Yet she has set out, quite deliberately, to cover up her Administration's nakedness by wrapping herself in the Falklands bunting, by belligerence of language, by a simplistic invocation of the Falklands spirit in the totally different sphere of industrial relations, and by a wish to turn a service of remembrance into a glorification of war. As she plans her parade she should learn that there is a difference between patriotism and jingoism.

This Government has forfeited any moral claim to the allegiance of the people. It has broken faith with the electorate.

If the Alliance is to provide new hope, it must restore faith in the capacity of the democratic political process. Our Alliance must provide new leadership, and fresh integrity. We start with a determination to put our country back to work.

Back to Work is indeed the title of the imaginative programme adopted enthusiastically by this Assembly earlier in the week: it signals a return to the economics of commonsense and ends the nonsense of paying people *not* to work when there is so much to do. Over three years we will take one million people off the dole queues and get this country moving again.

First, we will start a selective programme of capital spending, increasing the public investment level which by this year has shrunk to a mere 2% of current Gross Domestic Product. We shall invest in the future as well as the present, with vital public expenditure; on homes in urgent need of renovation; on schemes of energy conservation; on long-overdue improvement and electrification of our railways; and on encouraging the emerging high technology industries.

These will not merely be nationally inspired projects but will include a whole range of regional and local schemes. Take just one example. In Manchester, the city's sewerage system is falling apart, literally. There have been over fifty major collapses in the central area alone since 1975. There are thirty-five miles of tunnels that need replacing. This one urgent project would generate some 4,000 jobs.

Second, we will re-activate the economy by cutting away the restraints upon our competitiveness and on business. We will bring down interest rates by operating a competitive exchange rate and joining the European Monetary System.

We will scrap the National Insurance Surcharge — the iniquitous tax on jobs so loved by Denis Healey and Geoffrey Howe alike.

But we will introduce also a series of measures designed to boost small businesses. In the short term that will provide the most realistic boost for jobs in the private sector.

Third, we will initiate a massive training effort to give all young people under 18 the chance of at least eight hours a week training; and, at the other end of the scale, we will extend the Job Release Scheme to the over 60s.

Fourth, we will greatly expand the programme of job creation, in particular for the long-term unemployed. There is much work to be done to improve our environment and our social services.

Now of course, all this will mean spending more money and expanding the Public Sector Borrowing Requirement. After the savings on unemployment and social security benefit, and the increased tax revenue from those newly in work, the net cost carefully checked on the Treasury's own computer will be £3,000 million a year for three years.

But there will be no long-term benefit to the economy if this extra spending merely fuels inflation. The fundamental difference between the Labour Party's proposals and those of the Alliance is our firm belief in the anchor which will stop this recovery drifting into the whirlpool of inflation. That anchor is a sustainable incomes policy.

Establishing a fair, firm and sustainable incomes policy will not be easy. Without it we are lost. The Tories would accelerate the haemorrhage of job losses and Labour would put us into terminal decline, unable to hold back runaway inflation. As the *Guardian* put it: "without wage restraint Labour's package spells inflationary disaster".

We will have no truck with that pathetically familiar feature of British economic and political life; the pre-election consumer boom. Even now the cabinet is planning tax cuts next spring, sweeteners for the voters. The result of this electoral bribery will be to suck in more imported cars, more imported washing machines, more imported TV sets — and with each import more British jobs will be exported.

By contrast, we are planning for investment-led recovery, striking at unemployment while resisting the corrosive force of inflation. We shall fight doctrinaire privatisation by the Tories as fiercely as we have fought doctrinaire nationalisation by Labour. British industry desperately needs a period of stability.

It needs active and constructive help too. Yet as Liberals we know that however helpful government policy may be, nothing will be achieved without a change of attitude at work.

Will the way in which management and employees face the future be positive, energetic and imaginative, adjusting to changes in technology and responding to our competitors? Or will it be surly and negative, concerned to protect the past and shut the door on the future?

Of course all parties are concerned with this vital question. Yet Labour and Tories alike have come up with the wrong answers. Labour believe that the bureaucrats in Whitehall and Trade Union bosses at the TUC can change attitudes. Tories believe that it is enough to appeal to the profit motive of a few investors.

Liberals have the right answer, the human answer. It is partnership. We need a revolution in industrial relations in Britain. The Nissan Company has said that they are reluctant to build a car plant in Britain because British workers couldn't understand that managers were human beings who wanted to mix freely on the shop floor. It would be difficult they said to introduce Japanese methods of communication between workers and management necessary for higher productivity because of the historical conflict between different classes that characterise British society.

That is precisely what we Liberals have always said. I hope Mrs Thatcher listened when she was in Tokyo instead of taking advantage of Japanese politeness to give one of her little homilies.

To us partnership is not just a pious hope or a management technique. It is the moral basis of a Liberal society. Free people — sharing adversity when it is necessary. Sharing the rewards of their labour and sharing decisions. That is why we shall change company law to turn the limited concept of companies owned by capital alone into living organisations which represent a genuine community of interest of all who contribute to them.

It must be the same with our politics too. When we talk about the new politics, we mean really giving democracy a chance. We want a government, ministers and civil servants alike, which is genuinely accountable to parliament and open to public scrutiny. We want a House of Commons which truly represents the people of this country. We want a constitution which protects the rights of individuals, which pushes power back to the communities of Britain and which guards the rule of law.

It is a curious thing that this country which gave birth to parliamentary democracy has got stuck with a very limited nineteenth century version of it. Now we want to extend democracy and use it to breathe life back into our tired institutions.

We are committed to a Scottish parliament and to devolution of power in the rest of the United Kingdom. We have reaffirmed our total commitment to the introduction of proportional representation. I do not want anyone to underrate our seriousness. Make no mistake, the Alliance will not compromise on this fundamental democratic reform.

But we cannot be concerned with Britain alone. We live in a troubled world, and I fear that the instinctive response to its huge problems is isolation, mutual suspicion and narrow nationalism.

We are beset by problems: of trade, of declining economic activity, or a dangerous fragility in banking and financial arrangements. Over everything looms the growing calamity of world poverty: of famine, scarce resources and over-population.

The Brandt Report struck a ready and enthusiastic popular chord, yet the response of governments was frankly inadequate. At the international summit in Mexico the problems were tossed aside. A bland and pious communiqué was the only outcome.

An even greater scandal of our age is the sordid traffic in conventional arms, and the insanity of the nuclear arms race. I understand why so many people have been moved by the build up of nuclear weapons to campaign actively for disarmament. But there has been little tangible result. This summer, five weeks of talks at the United Nations, including speeches from many of the world's leaders, culminated in the unmitigated failure of the Second Special Session on Disarmament.

There are some things we can do on our own. We can abandon the pretence of a British independent deterrent. We can and we will cancel the Trident project. But that is not enough. We need effective international agreement. That is why I place so much store on real progress at the multilateral disarmament talks at Geneva. Success there is not helped by those who talk of the possibility of fighting and "winning" a nuclear war. That is a fantastic illusion and dangerous nonsense. It would indeed be a war without winners.

But as we have seen in recent days nuclear war is not the only horror which threatens mankind.

The terrible devastation of Beirut culminating in the unspeakable barbarism of last month's massacre, deserves more than mere condemnation of those directly responsible. It also demands a recognition by many nations, including Britain, of our own complicity — in fuelling the Middle East conflict by an unrelenting and cynical traffic in arms to both sides. We will lead a European initiative to dam the flood of arms to that unhappy region.

On my own overseas visits last year, in particular Washington, Peking and the UN itself I have become more and more convinced that we

Liberals must work for a new International Charter, as fundamental and far-reaching as the post-war settlement, which included Bretton Woods and the foundation of the UN.

In the United States the Democratic Party has proposed a mutual and verifiable freeze on the manufacture and deployment of all nuclear weapons, leading therefore step by step to the creation of nuclear-free zones, the reduction of existing stockpiles and thence to general disarmament.

This year too the Palme Commission has put forward a host of practical measures for real disarmament, including battlefield nuclear free zones.

As we cut back on arms spending, the billions of pounds saved should be utilised for the development of the Third World. Growth and prosperity in those areas, which are so desperately poor at present, could provide a great engine to get the world's economy moving again.

In parallel the Charter should define a new set of relationships to cover finance, monetary systems and resources in such a way that equity and efficiency replace corruption and chaos.

A new international settlement of this sort must involve the Soviet bloc and China. It is formidably difficult but no-one can seriously doubt that it is necessary.

In working for this the European Community has a particular responsibility and opportunity. Britain should share the leadership of the community and our government will not behave like this one, complaining about them all being out of step with us. Not for nothing is our Prime Minster known throughout the continent as la belle dame sans merci.

Looking at the state of the world today and at Britain itself it is no wonder that so many young people have become disillusioned or disaffected. I want particularly to say a few words to them today:

Standing aside, nursing a grievance, will change nothing. Come and join us. You need us to end the drift and shatter the complacency of the old politics, and we need you to help us do it.

But I want to appeal as well to those who are older and more established: Don't write off a whole generation. Young people and their ideas must be given a chance. This generation should be of special concern. We have a generation of young people, who are bright, well educated and highly motivated. Yet the missing factor for them that was always there for those of us brought up in the post-war period is hope. We have bred a generation almost without hope, who can echo the poet:

> *"Ah what shall I be at fifty*
> *Should nature keep me alive*
> *If I find the world so bitter*
> *When I am but twenty-five."*

Our embittered young see us spending billions on more and more sophisticated weapons while poverty and ignorance continue; they see us willing and able to fight a war eight thousand miles away, but unwilling or unable to find the same amounts of money and effort to tackle the things that matter to them: their education, their jobs and their chance for a decent life.

The anguish in the voice of our young people is also a protest of individuality against uniformity; what Goethe called "the deadly commonplace that fetters us all". Our amorphous bureaucracy and our insensitive institutions are fetters which the young wish to throw off. We should listen carefully to their protest. We will be judged by our reactions.

What they want is not the easy half-truths and euphemisms about "bottoming out" or "turning the corner". They don't want lecturing or hectoring from a Prime Minister: they want understanding.

We can link the idealism of youth to the fine liberal traditions of individual worth, of tolerance, of dissent, of democratic change. Let us make their demand for a limitation on the abuse of power ours as well; let us embrace their demand for a new politics which enhances the quality of life, gives the individual dignity, yet preserves our sense of community. They want a government that speaks directly and honestly to its citizens and one that listens as well, and that is what we are going to give them.

We are a new force in British politics which is realistic, purposeful, and above all hopeful. We must campaign with all our strength and conviction between now and the election.

We represent a new kind of leadership which is not imprisoned by class or ideology or sectional interest. We offer a new kind of politics which truly represents all the people.

That is the real significance of the Alliance. Just as we have brought Liberals and Social Democrats together in a common cause, we must now bring people and government together in a new alliance. Partnership and teamwork are what we believe in. Equality of sacrifice in the hard times is what we shall insist on. Equality of reward when we win through will be the right of every citizen.

Making this country a decent place to live in for all of us will not be easy. But if it is not done together it will not be done at all. Carry this message into every city, every town and every village of these islands. Don't despair. Cut free from the past.

I have one last quotation from this discredited document. It puts in a sentence the prevailing philosophy of the Conservative Party: "government strategies and plans cannot produce revival".

You see, they abdicated the proper responsibility of government even before they took office. This is a do nothing, care less government.

That was not the attitude of Lloyd George and the Liberal Party in our Yellow Book of 1929, *We can conquer unemployment*. It was not the attitude of President Roosevelt when he adopted the same ideas in the New Deal which pulled America out of the slump of the Thirties. And it is not the attitude of the Liberal Party and our allies today.

So at the end of this Assembly we say to the Government: There *is* an alternative. We stand determined, united.

If you are not willing to act, we are.

If you do not care, we do.

If you will not give the people of this country the leadership they deserve, you should go.

We are ready to govern.

1983

Into battle at the General Election.

Chapter Eight

Know what you fight for

As the inevitable General Election approached, the Alliance had a lucky by-election break, not unlike that provided by Liverpool Edge Hill shortly before the 1979 election.

Bob Mellish, the Labour MP for the dockland seat of Southwark Bermondsey, had long been unhappy with a growing left-wing influence within his local Labour Party and had hinted at departure for more productive pastures, having first collected his peerage on the way out.

No sooner had these signals begun to be broadcast around the corridors of the Palace of Westminster then they were picked up by David Steel, who cajoled the Liberal Party Organisation into re-vamping the near-derelict Bermondsey Liberal Association and encouraging its few members to select a new and energetic prospective Liberal candidate, Simon Hughes.

This political investment paid off. The seat duly became vacant and the row over the controversial selection of Peter Tatchell as Labour candidate boiled over with the Labour 'old guard' in the constituency putting up a rebel Independent candidate, backed by the former MP.

At the end of a bruising campaign involving the highly distasteful vilification of Mr. Tatchell, principally by his erstwhile party colleague Mr. O'Grady, the opinion polls revealed that it was Hughes, and not O'Grady who was the challenger. Two years of assiduous community campaigning had paid off and in the last few days the bandwagon and the full power of the popular press swung behind Simon Hughes, who stormed to victory with 58% of the vote.

The result at Bermondsey provided the Alliance with the fillip it was so desperately seeking. By contrast, Labour was in trouble. Michael Foot, the Labour leader, having originally and rather ineffectually disowned Peter Tatchell, was partly blamed for the debacle and also had to taste the bitter fruits of defeat.

Ironically, the position was nearly reversed only a few months later at the Darlington by-election. There it was the SDP candidate, Tony Cook, who began as the clear favourite but the moderate Labour candidate, Ossie O'Brien, who steadily gained ground.

For the Alliance, the campaign was as disastrous in Darlington as it had been successful in Bermondsey. Labour won the seat convincingly and the Alliance trailed in a poor third, with the hapless Cook the principal scapegoat. Significantly, Labour's tenure proved shortlived, with the seat succumbing to the Tory landslide which shortly was to come.

In May, on the evidence of a commanding lead in the opinion polls, the Prime Minister asked the Queen for the dissolution of Parliament.

Nonetheless, the Alliance entered the campaign with some confidence. In the eleven by-elections between June 1981 and December 1982, Liberals and Social Democrats had polled 31% of the vote — equal to that polled by the official opposition, and only 1% behind the Conservative Government. Despite the 'Falklands factor' their standing in the polls — hovering around the 20% mark — represented a higher starting point than the Liberals had enjoyed in previous elections in recent memory; and, on past experience, David Steel had every expectation that the Alliance would be able to build its support steadily as polling day approached. There seemed everything to play for.

True, there were three remaining areas of difficulty and embarrassment — constituencies where, despite every threat and plea, rival candidates intended to battle it out. The results in the seats of Liverpool Broadgreen, Hammersmith, and Hackney South and Shoreditch, were to demonstrate the futility of such internecine conflict.

As the campaign drew to a close, there were signs that the long-awaited upward movement in the polls for the Alliance had begun. Yet as morning dawned on Friday, 10 June, the devastating reality of the results became apparent.

Labour had done disastrously, with its national vote plunging to

8,456,000, barely ahead of the Alliance. Compromised over its nuclear disarmament policy (previously considered the great vote winner) and lacking leadership appeal, the Party could scarcely muster 27% of the vote.

For their part, the SDP and the Liberals had polled 25.4% — well over 7½ million votes — which represented the best result since the 1923 election when the Liberals had scored 29.7% of the votes cast.

But once again it was the electoral system — as much as the efforts of its opponents — which dealt the Alliance a cruel blow. In 1923 a marginally higher share had netted the Liberals 158 seats; even with 23% of the vote in 1929 the Liberals under Lloyd George had won 59 seats. But in 1983 the final tally was just 23 Members of Parliament.

For the Liberals the by-election gain at Southwark and Bermondsey was held comfortably, although Bill Pitt was unable to contain the Tory tide in Croydon North-West. Five seats were gained. One was the new constituency of Roxburgh and Berwickshire (carved out of David Steel's old constituency, and with his protégé, Archy Kirkwood, a former Personal Assistant, as the candidate). Montgomery, lost in 1979 after almost 100 years of continuous Liberal representation, was won back from the Conservatives by 668 votes. Yeovil, in the West Country, and Gordon, in the hinterland of Aberdeen, were both gains from the Conservatives; and Michael Meadowcroft took Leeds West from Labour.

The SDP faced a more difficult problem. At the time of its formation it had enjoyed an enormous media 'hype', partly through the formation of an instant and glittering SDP Parliamentary Party very largely composed of defecting Labour MPs. Nearly all had made the conscious decision not to re-offer themselves to their respective electorates at that time under their new guise, but to await the General Election.

Inevitably, the special electoral vulnerability of SDP MPs had an adverse effect on the encouraging advance that SDP candidates, in parallel with the Liberals, were able to make in all parts of the country.

Emphasis was put on the fact that only five of the sitting SDP MPs escaped electoral oblivion, with Shirley Williams and Bill Rodgers the major casualties. While apparently a disaster, the retention of five seats coupled with the capture of the one-time Liberal seat of Ross and Cromarty (with the Isle of Skye now added) was, to those with a more realistic appreciation of the difficulties, a better result than some had feared. Appearances — like at the SDP's launch — were once again deceptive, but this time to the detriment of the new Party.

The hard truth was that the Alliance had polled well — but not well enough. Undoubtedly, the electoral effect of the Alliance had been to lift the vote markedly in areas where the Liberals on their own had polled poorly in the past. But in those crucial marginal seats where Liberal candidates had built themselves into a challenging position, the Alliance added little to offset the modest loss of former Liberal votes to the Conservatives — by those objecting to the Liberal link-up with what they saw as 'Socialists'.

The consequence was an impressive vote, evenly spread across the country, with only eleven Alliance lost deposits, but with little tangible parliamentary reward.

The Conservatives under Mrs. Thatcher, facing a fragmented opposition, had sustained the loss of half a million votes and, as David Steel put it, had polled the lowest Conservative vote since Bonar Law — but had nonetheless won a crushing landslide of Parliamentary seats.

In the aftermath of such a disappointing result, David Steel retired to lick his wounds. Physically drained, and suffering from influenza he faced a moment of deep despair. The unhelpful behaviour of some of his Party members, both during and after the election, had particularly upset him.

He had never been attracted to the idea of spending a political lifetime crying in the wilderness. His interest was in political power — and yet, despite all his efforts, that goal seemed as far removed as ever.

He therefore resolved to take a three-month sabbatical from the Leadership, to contemplate his political future. In that brooding period of personal re-examination, few realised how close he came to resigning the Liberal leadership.

And yet his self-imposed isolation was not total. In July, a Parliamentary by-election was held to fill the Penrith and the Border seat, formerly held by the freshly-ennobled Viscount Whitelaw. The seat adjoined David Steel's former constituency (before boundary changes) and he slipped over the border three times to join a by-election campaign which lacked the brilliant organisation of so many because most Liberals were also suffering post-election exhaustion. The voters, who had a month earlier returned Willie Whitelaw with a 15,000 majority, registered their marked unhappiness at being treated in so casual a fashion by the Government. The Tory candidate scraped home by 500 votes, barely ahead of Michael Young, the Liberal.

It was a sign of things to come. That September delegates to the Annual Liberal Assembly gathered in the comfortable Yorkshire town of Harrogate. Once again, all eyes were on the Leader's speech at the end of Conference Week, but this time his arrival in town was awaited with particular anxiety. Had David Steel got over his post-election 'blues'? Was he really fighting fit and willing to lead the Party through to the next election — or was his heart no longer in it?

As he began his speech, some of the tensions and frustrations of the Summer welled to the surface:

> As you may have heard I took a few days off this summer. But I'm back now and I must say you're all looking a good deal better for it. I did notice that during my absence my own rating in the Gallup poll reached record levels. There must be a moral in this somewhere.
>
> A saw this week that another party leader was asked by a reporter whether her hectic day trip to Holland had been too much for her. She replied, and I quote: "It might be too much for a normal person, but after all it is me", or as Miss Piggy would say, "c'est moi". Talking of The Muppet Show reminds me, I must thank Alan Beith for looking after the parliamentary party in my absence.
>
> But seriously, I am sure you will agree from what you have seen at this Assembly how lucky Alan as Chief Whip and I as Leader are to have such talented new additions to our team.
>
> This 1983 Assembly meets three months after a general election which has seen the return of the largest Liberal Party in the House of Commons since 1935. For our Alliance it was the largest third party vote since 1923. We have made a remarkable climb back from our seven hundred thousand votes in the 1951 election to our seven and a half million votes on June 9th this year.
>
> So my first words must be of warm congratulation to everyone in the party who has contributed to this achievement. I have had a chance to thank many of you personally in the last few days. But for those outside this hall who supported us so magnificently during the campaign — my heartfelt thanks. Of course we still have a long way to go to reach power — the power to implement Liberal policies — but another leap forward at the next election, of the same size as this last one, will see us there.
>
> For let this be clearly understood, the scale of our achievement has been masked only by the cruel distortions of our electoral system. In what other democracy could the official opposition poll 27.6 per cent of the popular vote and get 209 seats while our Alliance polling just 2 per cent less got only 23? In what other democracy could the Government suffer a loss of support of 1½ per cent of those voting, polling the lowest Conservative vote since Bonar Law, and yet end up with such an increased majority

capable of being described wholly incorrectly as a "landslide" in their favour?

I warn Tory and Labour politicians as they sit and manipulate a House of Commons which is now wholly unrepresentative of popular opinion that they go on doing so at their peril. A democracy which is deliberately insensitive to the real changes in public feeling sows the seeds of its own destruction. As I found on the doorsteps in the Penrith by-election, and as our remarkable vote there showed, there is now an enormous wave of public sympathy and support for the cause of electoral justice.

And I also warn them that while we fully support the all party Campaign for Fair Votes, we Liberals are not going to sit around whingeing: "We was robbed". It is my intention that we regroup and mobilise our forces to go on to win the next election under the present system and then to change it.

It has been said that the weakness of our Alliance is that our vote was evenly spread; that we piled up 313 second places throughout the land but that our vote was insufficiently concentrated in specific areas. That may be a short-term weakness but I believe it to be our long-term strength. We *do* appeal to *all* ages and classes and regions.

That is something neither of the other parties can any longer claim. How can the Tory party possibly pretend to be a genuinely national party when with their inflated majority they cannot muster a single MP in the great cities of Glasgow or Liverpool?

The Labour Party has been almost wiped out throughout the whole of the south of England below the London to Bristol line. There is one other feature of the last election which is highly significant and merits greater recognition. Ever since 1950 the Liberal Party has been caricatured as the lost deposit party. In that election we lost 319 deposits and Labour lost none. At this election we lost just five Liberal deposits — the same number as the Conservative Party. But Labour candidates lost their deposits in 119 constituencies. The mould of British politics may not have been smashed at this election, but we have cracked it beyond repair and it will not be used again.

What does that mean for us? First and foremost it means we must learn to start to look like a potential government. It means that without question our Alliance with the SDP must continue. The sight of two parties working together for the common good for the first time since the war has had dramatic impact. It must not only continue but develop organically and democratically at every level. Inevitably at the beginning of the Alliance a lot of ad hoc decisions had to be made at the top. Now we must move on from that.

It means developing policy with our allies over the next few years instead of waiting till the manifesto drafting period. We have set an example already in Parliament by creating groups to co-ordinate policy.

We must let the local friendships and partnerships, forged in the election, grow stronger. But at the same time, our proper commitment to decentralisation should not go so far as to leave us looking like a loosely knit rag bag with people free to act against the spirit of the Alliance in their region, city or constituency. The Alliance has meant and will mean taking and accepting some tough decisions.

We have worked out a way of fighting European seats together which will require us to respect each other's rules but which I am sure will be successful. In the coming discussions on Westminster seats we must be careful not to upset the excellent local understanding which now exists in the great majority of constituencies by initiating any attempt at a general reshuffle.

In the relatively small number of constituencies where either Liberals or Social Democrats seek change, it is essential that both parties face up to the obligation of sorting things out together fairly and locally. That is the way to avoid another round of national involvement and intervention.

But important as "who fights which seat" may be to the two parties of the Alliance, it is not what matters to the voters. They want to know and they are entitled to know whether the Alliance has worked out answers to the growing problems of Britain. That means that we must think together and we must campaign together on the great issues of our country's future. I want the Liberal Party to be a Thinking and Campaigning Party. I want us to be a Thinking and Campaigning Alliance.

Between 1974 and 1979 the Tory privateers captured the political debate. They imposed their ideas upon the national agenda.

Now it is up to us to recapture the intellectual initiative. Their ideas have proved impractical and their ideology barren, but it is up to us to show what we can do better. We must redefine and sharpen up our policies in a way that is both adventurous and responsible. We must command the debate.

Our policies must be developed step by step with our allies over the coming years. We must not be afraid to hammer out our differences. We must be willing to advance new plans and ideas which draw upon the traditions of Liberalism and Social Democracy to solve the crisis of our time. Like Keynes and Beveridge in their day we must be innovative and ambitious. The Tories believe they have so cowed the British people that all sense of confidence has ebbed away. 'A frightened nation is a conservative nation', they say to themselves.

We must prove them wrong by being prepared to put forward bold and radical plans for the renewal of Britain, and we must campaign vigorously upon them. I am determined that the very special style of campaigning which Liberals have developed so successfully over the past two decades should not be confined to local issues.

The Party in the Alliance must take its case to the people. We must take our campaign for the renewal of Britain into every home in this country with a message that will re-kindle the hope which Tory policies have done so much to destroy.

It is to the contents of that campaign that I want to devote my attention today. Over these next four years we must work together in five key areas of policy, to sharpen our impact.

I begin with the economy. In a speech during the election Sir Geoffrey Howe had the nerve to claim "we have created and will maintain a stable economic environment. Business confidence and employment opportunities are growing." Scarcely a day of the election passed without some Tory minister assuring us that recovery was just round the corner or that light had been sighted at the end of the tunnel. We now know that the June recovery was an illusion. How bitterly I find CBI members resenting that their leaders were swept along in the Tory euphoria.

This month the National Institute of Economic and Social Research told us that the growth expected in the economy over the next 18 months would be "too low to make any mark on unemployment." This Government, faced with the problems of a world recession, has deliberately used unemployment as its sole means to control inflation. By cutting public expenditure they have reduced productive economic activity and added an extra British recession on top of the world one.

The Government's financial targets for 1983 are the most restrictive of any of the big seven Western economies. The Tories cannot deny that since they took office in 1979 our industrial production has slumped seven times faster than the OECD average. Over the same period Britain had by far the worst record on overall output of all the 24 OECD member states.

The National Institute's report goes on to say "it is difficult to see a significant and national reduction in unemployment taking place without a fairly substantial stimulus". That is precisely what we called for before and during the election and we do so again today.

I must make it clear that when we oppose Tory economic policies and present our own alternatives we are not just talking of detailed changes here and there. We are saying that the present economic policies stem from a crude political philosophy that we Liberals find socially irresponsible and wholly unacceptable. Today's Tories are fired with the Friedmanite view that human improvement can only be achieved by unrelieved competition. We reject that view.

So do a long list of Tories who nowadays sound like a roll call from distant history: Soames, Gilmour, Carrington, Pym. The Prime Minister instead surrounds herself with the new hard-faced men who share her failed dogmas: Lawson, Brittan, Parkinson, Tebbit. I hear the BBC is trying to negotiate for a series of documentaries on the workings of cabinet. I have a title ready for them if they succeed: "Yes Prime Minister."

But it is a tragedy, not a comedy. The new Thatcher Tories are like the Prime Minister herself totally out of touch with the harsh reality of the life they have created for many of our people. I say they are out of touch because I believe that is true of leading Tories today. The only other and much less charitable explanation is that they *do* know and don't care.

The number of families caught in the poverty trap has doubled since they came to power four years ago. The Government's lack of concern about this reminds me of the Victorian Archbishop of Dublin who suggested to the Poor Law Enquiry Commission that all paupers should be tattooed on the foot or some other place so as to deter them from begging or receiving additional relief. He also suggested that any female receiving relief should have her hair cut off, pointing out with true devotion to the market economy that a good head of hair would fetch from 5 to 10 shillings, which represented a fortnight's maintenance. These are the Victorian values we can do without.

Whole areas of our great cities are so riddled with unemployment that we now have a law and disorder problem of serious proportions. Our newspapers week by week bring us reports from the courts of suicides brought on by failure to find work. NHS prescriptions for sedative drugs have shown an alarming and costly increase in areas of high unemployment. The picture of despair among the young who've never had a job is matched only by the prematurely retired people in their 50s who fear they will never work again.

Let the Prime Minister listen to the words of her great predecessor Disraeli instead of the false prophets she has been following: "It is community of purpose that constitutes society. Without that men may be drawn into contiguity but they still continue virtually isolated". It is that community of purpose which is so devastatingly lacking in the philosophy of this Government — leading to the creation of two nations between whom Disraeli saw "no intercourse and no sympathy; who are as ignorant of each other's habits, thoughts and feelings as if they were inhabitants of different plants". That is the main achievement of the Thatcher philosophy today. She and her advisers have perverted the Liberal concept of liberty. We believe that unless participation in the fullness of life in our country is treated as a right for all, liberty remains an empty word, a pretty veil behind which privilege may thrive.

So our first duty as an Alliance must be to advocate constructive ways of putting people back to work. And the second priority for the Alliance is the maintenance and revival of our country's public assets. The way they have been eroded by the Tories is a scandal. Because of our Liberal inheritance from the days of Lloyd George we are particularly incensed at the erosion of our health and social services.

The Tories have partly succeeded in persuading our people that as a nation we have been living in the lap of luxury enjoying benefits in excess of other countries and which we cannot afford. This is just not true. I found when I was in Canada during the summer that our Liberal colleagues there spend more of their Gross National Product on health than we do. They have more doctors and more hospital beds than we do per 1000 population. The same is true of Australia.

What economic and social lunacy it is to have empty wards, longer waiting lists, and nurses and ancillary workers drawing unemployment benefit. What a tragedy that at a time of falling school rolls and empty classrooms we should have teachers in the dole queue instead of improving the quality of our education by reducing class sizes.

The crude and intermittent financial attacks on our universities and colleges have meant the abandonment of the right to higher education which all post 1960 governments until this one supported. We have been failing to invest in our material infrastructure and in private industry. To add on top of these the failure to invest in the skill of our people for the future is disgraceful.

Mrs Thatcher claims to be a disciple of Winston Churchill, but she is highly selective in her knowledge of him, for in his book "The People's Rights" he dealt at length with the need for the public utilities and went on to say that "the State must increasingly and earnestly concern itself with the care of the sick and aged, and above all, of the children".

Today's Tories are doing the very reverse, and in the process frittering away the benefits of our greatest contemporary asset, North Sea oil. Let us therefore in our Alliance renew our faith in the public assets of this country — our railways, airports, road network; our coal, gas, electricity, steel and shipbuilding, to replace public shoddiness with public pride.

The industrial world may be running out of jobs in the ordinary sense, but it is certainly not running out of work. There is plenty waiting to be done — enough to restore everybody's self-respect and give meaning to their lives.

There is a lot of nonsense talked about the wisdom of growth, about this country having to choose between jobs and the environment. Mrs. Thatcher has proved that isn't true. She has succeeded in destroying both at the same time.

On the contrary, the right investment in the repair and rehabilitation of this country could get the economy moving, get people back to work and enhance and conserve our precious physical environment for future generations.

There is a massive job to be done in reclaiming our inner cities, in repairing, insulating and refurbishing old housing stock, in cleaning up urban wastelands and building new parks and playing fields. That's the way to get the construction industry moving again, not by building a new rash of commuter towns deep in the Green Belt.

Yet Mrs. Thatcher cannot escape from the prison of her own ideology. For her, energy use can only be limited by putting prices up. For her, land is a commodity to be bought and sold by her friends in the City, not a precious national asset. For her, public investment is anathema — even if it helps encourage private industry to get going again.

So we have been condemned to another four years of these squalid and short-sighted policies which will leave a landscape of dereliction behind them, with concrete where there should be green fields and city slums where there should be thriving communities.

The opportunity to use this time of economic crisis to create a more sustainable society is there for the taking. We must do it before the North Sea oil runs out, poured away by a deeply irresponsible government on a wave of imported foreign goods.

I want future generations to look back and say: This, our generation of political leadership, had the sense and foresight to build a country which is fit for us to inherit.

My third theme is that we must search for an enhanced role for the individual in our society. "Less government" is a legitimate demand in our over-bureaucratic society. It means more autonomy for individuals, groups, regions, businesses, organisations, decentralised groups of all kinds. We Liberals have long proclaimed the need for partnership in industry. The message is catching on slowly but surely, yet we have still not given this subject the priority it deserves. We should spell out the advantages of our policy in far more dramatic terms.

Why for a start should we not require all nationalised industries to operate genuine industrial partnership? One of the most original speeches at the TUC this year was made by Bill Sirs, the leader of the Iron and Steel Trades Confederation, when he said that the labour movement had with the best of intentions created monsters out of the public industries. "Under nationalisation", he said, "we the shareholders have no mechanism for controlling them at all". He is absolutely right. I believe the whole public sector would be much more efficient if those who work in it were given a proper say in its running. Indeed where possible, as in British Leyland, a cash share in its increased productivity and success. That is the way to greater prosperity for the nation and satisfaction for the workforce.

In the private sector the government should not *order* industry into new forms of organisation but it should give far larger tax carrots for those who switch to approved partnership schemes. We should as a movement study and publicise those firms like Baxi Heating who have in recent years successfully adopted partnership principles, and look at experience overseas. In America for example the airline People's Express makes it a prior condition of employment that you own at least 100 shares in the company and if you haven't got the money they will let you pay by instalments out of your wages. The chairman of the company declares that everyone in his company is a manager. Everyone makes between a quarter and half their basic salary through profit sharing. The firm operates with half the usual ratio of employees to aircraft and the result is lower fares for the customer.

Let us inject some zeal into our advocacy of these policies. It is only through them that we can for example get an incomes policy generally accepted as a more civilized method of controlling inflation than unemployment. It is only through industrial partnership that we will break down the class barriers which so bedevil our national life and which are in the interests of the Conservative and Labour parties to maintain. It is only in an atmosphere of co-operation that we will get people to face the necessary re-appraisal of work in the face of the new technologies.

One of the central issues of the world of tomorrow is how do we transform our dependence on jobs into a wider dependence on activity, including part-time work, education, leisure and voluntary assistance in developing the otherwise costly personal social services in an ageing society. Our Alliance parties still have a great deal of thinking to undertake in this area.

My fourth theme is that our Alliance demonstrates a coherent and well thought out concern for our future human environment, and especially the health of local government as the main agency for securing this.

A deep concern for the individual is the heart of our approach. But that means safeguarding his liberties and rights from bureaucratic intrusion; it means exercising a firm control over the pace of technological change so that the new technology remains our servant and not our master; it means giving the citizen rights of access to information; it means proper protection for ethnic and other minorities — giving equality before the law, providing equality of opportunity, whether in education or in work, and welcoming cultural diversity. Let us live up to our Party's constitutional aim that none should be enslaved by a narrow mass conformity.

And it means rejecting those who would impose a set blueprint of what constitutes human happiness whether that be the product of Tory paternalism or State socialism.

That is why a responsive, open and alive system of local democracy is so important. But over the last four years we have seen a relentless assault on local government, with a procession of White Papers, legislative proposals and a maze of mind-numbing and unworkable financial formulae. These financial controls are imposed with no regard to the human consequences, and are constraints which central Government would not dream of accepting in Whitehall. Of course there may be provocation from authorities controlled by the Labour left. I have a peace proposal to make. Mrs. Thatcher should promise to stop trying to run the GLC if Ken Livingstone will stop trying to run the country.

The greatest damage has been caused to local government by forcing it to be an instrument of the Government's monetarist obsessions. My own regional council earlier this month warned me that maintenance of services in the Borders — our roads, bridges, school buildings — are gradually disintegrating.

There is a desperate need to spend more merely to get back to the standards of 10 years ago. But instead, the Government permits only a ludicrous 2.6 per cent for inflation next year. We all know that inflation is going to be much more than that. Therefore inevitably there will be a serious reduction in real terms in local authority services.

Now we have the latest proposals for ratecapping — hitting at the remaining power local authorities have to raise their own funds and set their own level of services. So my regional council cannot even remedy this disastrous position by its own actions. Is it any wonder that councillors feel there is little point in giving up their time in service to local government when it's so hamstrung by central government?

If we believe in local democracy, we are going to have to fight for it. We have our shock troops on the ground, 2,000 Liberal councillors ready to take the argument into their council chambers and on to the Government itself. Together our MPs and councillors must unfurl the banner of local freedom.

I now turn to the last of my five points, but by no means the least — the assertion of a new international role for Britain. Some say we found that role in the Falklands. We did not. I have been unstinting in my praise for our military achievement. We backed the expeditionary force because we backed the rule of law and the United Nations charter so brusquely ignored by the Argentine Junta. We paid a heavy price for those principles and for rescuing the Falkland Islanders from the cruel invasion. Some of our fellow citizens paid the ultimate price. The triumph was one in which we all shared.

But the ugly jingoism which once or twice surfaced in the Prime Minister's vocabulary during that war has led to the most outrageously futile policy in peace — that of fortress Falklands. Here we have a Government which at every turn tells us how it must limit public expenditure in every direction, seriously proposing to spend (on the garrison, on new airports and other services in the Islands) one and a half million pounds per Islander.

And what for? Such expenditure will not lead to permanent security or immunity from attack — only a political settlement can achieve that. And in any case, as a report I have just received from the Islands privately confirms, the conversion of the Islands into a military fortress threatens to ruin the very way of life of the Islanders which we are meant to be protecting.

Commonsense must prevail. The Argentine is due to return to democracy next autumn. We are alienating Latin America, the United States, and indeed the whole United Nations by our obdurate policy. Instead we should be make it clear that when democracy returns we will of course resume direct discussions with the Argentine for the long term future of the Islands. In the meantime, we should welcome any help from the U.N. or the Organisation of American States to establish international guarantees of their security. We are now paying too high a price for Mrs. Thatcher's vanity, and we shall say so loud and clear.

The international role for Britain is not and cannot be that of Britain ruling the waves. It should be of a Britain using her world-wide Commonwealth connections, her special relationship with the United States, her membership of the EEC and NATO, as a major force for peace, stability, arms control and a just distribution of resources in our troubled world. There is no need to be hesitant in assuming such a leadership. The background of mutual paranoia of the two super-powers rules them out of this task. We could assist in reducing these global tensions, suspicions and distrust by promoting political dialogue between East and West. It is scandalous that the Prime Minister prevented Francis Pym from doing that. Political summitry may have gone out of fashion, but I believe it is the quickest way to increase understanding and create a better atmosphere in which disarmament talks can operate.

We as a people have a common interest with both the Americans and the Russians in achieving major reductions in expenditure on nuclear weaponry. The Soviet Union spends two or three times as much of its gross national product on military purposes as the NATO powers. It does so inevitably at the expense of progress for its citizens. Military expenditure throughout the world over the last four years has been increasing at a rate of 4 per cent a year, twice the rate of the previous four years. This is an insanity which must be stopped, for as President Eisenhower once remarked, "Every gun that is made, every warship launched, every rocket fired, signifies in a final sense a theft from those who hunger and are not fed, from those who are cold and not clothed."

That is even more true of today's expensive hardware. Every week three hundred thousand people die of starvation, a death toll equivalent to two Hiroshimas a week. Assuredly the Brandt Report was correct in saying that the twin causes of disarmament and world development go hand in hand. Far from adopting its proposals, our Government has brazenly lopped a further 2 per cent off the already declining overseas budget since June. Governments which go round penny-pinching from the arts and overseas aid tell you something about what kind of tawdry values they have.

If they want to penny-pinch they might look instead at the fact that Britain has almost four times as many brigadiers, admirals and above for every 1,000 troops as the Americans, and all of them with increased salaries protected under this Government's special pay policy for top people.

But serious disarmament is not just a matter of economics, it is a matter of survival. Both sides build increasing numbers of nuclear weapons and stockpile them to prevent their use. There is a logical malfunction here somewhere. Nuclear war is unlikely — in my view — to come about because of political confrontation between the two superpowers. It is now much more likely by accident. The ill-fated Korean airliner had its course set by computer. The communications systems set between it and the Russian fighters were different. If tragedy occurred after a 2½ hour flight, how much more likely is error on the short missile flights between East and West. To err is human, but for a real cock-up you need a computer. So the stakes are high and getting higher, and the need for a sustained impetus for nuclear disarmament becomes the highest priority for the peoples of this world.

I am not saying that the creation of a new concept of common security is easy. I hope that those who think those nice Russians can lightly be persuaded to abandon their SS20 deployment programme will have thought again after the callous destruction of that Korean airliner. Even the latest Andropov proposals would leave the fire power of three thousand Hiroshima bombs directed at Western Europe.

But today the talks at Geneva stand at a critical point. The British Government's attitude and activities in the days and weeks ahead could make all the difference. There have been some hints of movement on the Soviet side in the talks recently. Our European Allies would welcome British pressure for constructive disarmament counter proposals from an American Administration which has too often seemed frozen in its own cold-war rhetoric. The trouble is that Mrs. Thatcher seems to be content to be President Reagan's echo rather than his ally. I don't want Britain to be the East Germany of the Atlantic Alliance.

One of the major obstacles to agreement at Geneva is the refusal of Britain to put Polaris into the Geneva equation. There has been no flicker of response from Britain to this not unreasonable suggestion. Why?

It is easy to see one reason why the Government is reluctant. If allowance is made today for the 192 Polaris warheads, allowance will have to be made tomorrow for the 896 Trident warheads. It would then become embarrassingly clear to everyone how this misbegotten Trident project would give a vicious upward twist to the nuclear arms race worldwide. We know already that this subject has become an obstacle to agreement in Geneva and yet, rather than abandon Trident, Her Majesty's Government is willing to put the Geneva talks at risk.

If we are confronted with the deployment of Cruise missiles this autumn, it will not only be the position that the Russians and the Americans have taken in the negotiations that will affect this Party's attitude. It will not just be the presence or absence of a dual key system. It will also be whether this Government has helped or hindered the prospects for peace by their conduct and policies over the coming crucial weeks.

There is a further major risk of nuclear war. It lies in the lesser powers indulging in conventional wars which get out of control. It is high time that the developed powers stopped whetting the appetites of these countries with arms sales promotions. The world is sadly full of Galtieris, Ghadafis, Begins, Bothas or Khomeinis whose aggressive concept of their national interest is to trample on the rights of others. That during this summer France should sell jet fighters equipped with Exocet missiles to Iraq, or that we should have sent a cross-Channel car ferry loaded as an arms sales exhibition round the Middle East is unforgivable. Did we learn nothing from our arms trade with the Argentine?

And as candid friend to President Reagan it is time the Prime Minister told him bluntly that we do not regard the harrassment of Nicaragua or the propping up of El Salvador as being the first line in the defence of human freedom.

Britain is in a unique position to be a new and vital force for world peace. We are determined to make her so.

If I try to sum up my five themes, they amount to a plea for us to listen to what people are telling us in Britain today. To listen to the cry of men and women who feel themselves the victims of blind economic and political forces beyond their control. To recognise the frustration of people excluded from the process of making decisions even over their own lives, the feeling of hopelessness and powerlessness to shape their own destinies.

The duty of our political movement is to display such conviction, imagination and responsibility that we establish ourselves as the mainstream reformers in touch with the feelings and aspirations of ordinary folk. We have to restore faith in democratic politics, and invite new recruits in to help us.

In my first speech to you as leader in 1976 I said that the road I intended us to travel back to power would be a bumpy one. And indeed we have climbed some rough terrain together. But look where we've got to. We have established for the first time in fifty years a really secure base camp. We are ready to begin the final assault on that summit.

First we must be *confident*. Confident of our cause and our chance of success. Confident in each other and in our allies.

Second we must be *united*. Healthy debate is essential. The party needs new ideas and vitality. But the time has come for us to operate more as a team, now and especially during the next election itself.

Third, and most important, we must be *far-sighted*. Liberals have always led the way in responding to new political opportunities with vision. That has never been more needed than now.

A timid, divided and short-sighted party would fail, and would deserve to fail because it would have lost its nerve. A confident, united and far-sighted Liberal Party will give the lead to the Alliance.

Politics is so often just about parties chasing after votes. Yet in contrast today we have the extraordinary phenomenon of the public seeking a movement worthy of their support. We must respond. We have clearly touched a chord in the hearts of the British people. Now we must build a new consensus, with an honourable role for our country. As we've seen in these last two years, to die for one's country is still recognised as noble. But to live and work for its best purposes is noble too.

We must re-define true patriotism. A Britain famous once more for its civilisation, competence and compassionate domestic leadership could be a forceful example in the quest for international order and justice.

Our party and our Alliance have an historic role to play in the renewal of Britain. It is our duty. It is expected of us. There is no limit to what we can achieve together if we believe in each other and in our cause.

I commend to you the words of Oliver Cromwell:

"know what you fight for and love what you know."

1984

"Ahem! Anybody mind if I take two months off for a rest!"

Chapter Nine

The three year haul

By the beginning of 1984, the dust of the General Election battle had cleared. Despite a drop in its overall vote, the Conservative Party had been returned to office with an electoral landslide of 144 seats in the new House of Commons. Mrs Thatcher reigned supreme, assured of another five years in Downing Street. Labour, though having lost the support of millions of its traditional voters, remained the official Opposition. The two-party system — despite the strongest third party challenge in fifty years — seemed to have re-asserted itself with a vengeance.

But, beneath the surface, a lot had changed. That was certainly true of the Alliance — and, some feared, of David Steel. The Liberal Leader had returned to British politics in the Autumn of 1983, after a three month sabbatical, seemingly refreshed and avowing his intention of leading the Liberal Party into the next election.

Yet doubts and rumours were to persist. The results of the General Election had been a desperate disappointment to him. The mould-breaking instrument, which David Steel personally had done so much to fashion, had promised much — but had failed in its task of breaking open the system and securing a realignment of British politics. Did David Steel now have the heart to continue? Could he withstand the rigour of the long haul?

There had been other changes in the Alliance, most notably in the leadership of the SDP. Four days after the 1983 election, on 13 June,

Roy Jenkins had announced his resignation as SDP Leader in these terms:

"I regard it as desirable that the SDP should immediately have a Leader for the next election. Fortunately, with David Owen's victory at Devonport, such a leader is available.

"It is for the SDP MPs to nominate and for the membership as a whole to make a decision. But I hope that David Owen may be elected without a contest, and will lead the Party to the full success that its solid basis in votes makes possible."

The man whom Roy Jenkins had defeated for the leadership two years earlier had now taken over and Roy Jenkins — former Chancellor of the Exchequer, Home Secretary and President of the European Commission — had returned to the backbenches, though, he assured the Party, "in no mood of defeat and dismay".

That change involved the Alliance in rather more than adjusting to a new SDP leader — although given David Owen's sometimes abrasive dynamism, his challenging intellect and his previous experience of high ministerial office (which naturally he drew upon freely), that in itself was not always easy.

While, after the comradeship of a common struggle, many Liberals favoured a merger of the two Alliance parties, David Owen was resolutely opposed to such a course. That was scarcely surprising. The Party had not been in existence for more than a few years. It had gone to some trouble to replicate the structures and trappings of a national party. It had a fresh and capable new Leader. And it feared that a hasty decision to merge with the numerically, organisationally and electorally stronger Liberals would be tantamount to surrender.

This mood of caution was understandable. In his farewell conference speech as Leader, Roy Jenkins, aware of this feeling, had also ruled out "premature and disruptive mergers". But he had gone on to warn SDP members not to "set a limit to the march of the Alliance". In other words, the habit of working together, with joint campaigning, joint policy-making and joint decision-making, could gradually make separate Party structures wasteful, unnecessary and irrelevant. It would be "organic merger".

David Steel and the Liberals could accept that much. But far more alarming was the impression given by David Owen, not only that merger was out of the question, now or in the future, but that a time might come, with the advent of proportional representation, when the Alliance might be no more and Liberals and Social Democrats would be no longer allies but competitors in the search for votes.

Other tensions were to arise — about the joint selection of candidates or about joint policy-making — which indicated that the Steel-Owen relationship — and the view that each took of the development of the Alliance — was to be very different from the benign and close partnership enjoyed by David Steel and Roy Jenkins.

David Steel was also aware of important changes closer to home — within the ranks of the Parliamentary Liberal Party itself. No less than seven of the seventeen-strong band of Liberal MPs were new to the House of Commons (including the victor of the Bermondsey by-election, Simon Hughes). Their experience as candidates — and some, as councillors — had led them to adopt a more corporate approach to politics than those MPs who had gone before.

The Parliamentary Liberal Party had never been much more than a dozen in number ever since 1945, and sometimes a lot less. While David Steel had all but eradicated the distressing tendency for even this small grouping to splinter in all directions when confronted with a Parliamentary vote, he had nonetheless resigned himself to his colleagues' mercurial and ragged individualism. After 1983, this began to change — with the weekly meeting of the Parliamentary Liberal Party becoming far more businesslike and productive.

Apart from these developments within the Alliance, British politics outwardly seemed remarkably unchanged. Indeed, the European elections in June seemed to reinforce that point, although only repeating the flagrant injustice which the electoral system had meted out a year earlier.

On a much lower turnout, Labour made modest gains from the Conservatives, providing some encouragement to the Party's new Leader, Neil Kinnock. However, the Alliance polled 19.5% of the vote, but failed to secure the election of a single Member of the European Parliament. Russell Johnston, who had won Inverness in great style at the General Election and whose victory in the Highlands and Islands Euro-Constituency was confidently predicted, was badly beaten by Winnie Ewing, the Scottish Nationalist. 5.4 million votes had elected 45 Conservative MEPs; just under half that number had provided the Alliance with no reward whatsoever.

The contrast was as cruel elsewhere in Europe as it was at home. In the Netherlands, 1 million votes had been sufficient to elect 5 MEPs; 2½ million votes in Britain elected nobody.

However, the Alliance had reason to be grateful for one welcome consolation prize. On the same day, at a Parliamentary by-election at Portsmouth South, popular local SDP Councillor Mike Hancock had stormed to victory with a majority of 1,341 over his Tory opponent. It provided the Alliance with a much needed boost and pointed the way to events to come.

The 1984 Liberal Assembly — held in Bournemouth once more — promised to be a challenging one for David Steel.

He faced the prospect of a damaging Party split over defence and nuclear weapons — and over cruise missiles, in particular.

He needed to provide the Party with political leadership on the broader front, at a time when Britain remained locked in a long-running and extremely bitter Miners' Strike. Confrontation politics had never seemed more in vogue.

And, with David Owen filling the headlines and the television screens, Steel had to assert his authority in the Alliance — and reassure his Party that he really was set for "the three year haul".

With talk of new rivals for his post as Leader, fuelled by bizarre press speculation, David Steel launched into his traditional Friday speech:

> Well we've had an interesting week. No one can say it has been dull.
>
> Even meetings of the parliamentary party have been enlivened by the babble of the bookies and the shouting of the odds. It's felt more like Newmarket on race day.
>
> I don't want to dampen anyone's enthusiasm but we won't be putting the runners under starters' orders yet. We have other important races to win first.
>
> Yesterday we had a debate of high quality on defence and disarmament. We have one area of disagreement among us on the best strategy for getting rid of cruise missiles and I do not seek to minimise it but, with that exception, we have agreed what I believe is the only party policy in Britain today which genuinely seeks to combine the needs of defence *and* disarmament. That is a policy for real security.
>
> And I was delighted that we so overwhelmingly rejected the call to come out of NATO and remove bases from the UK. Unlike the Labour Party we have fully committed ourselves to NATO as our defence shield. But this week we have also shown how NATO should take the way forward on disarmament and become an Alliance for peace. We will make our full contribution to that process by putting Polaris into the arms negotiations.
>
> Unlike Labour and the Conservatives we are internationalists committed to working with other countries and I welcome the strong emphasis in the resolution on strengthening the European pillar of NATO.
>
> We have agreed that by 1986 we will draw up our priorities for government. Meanwhile the military and political scene will have moved on, but I am confident that, looking at the principles of common security

and positive progress to peace agreed here this week, we shall be
successful, and that we shall go on to convince the electorate that it is
possible to combine hope and realism in defence policy.

Protection of green belts has been relaxed in favour of new speculative
development while many of our inner cities present a picture of destitution
and decay.

Above all, there is the continuing and worsening bloody battleground
which is laughably referred to as British industrial relations. Our national
crisis is not just an economic crisis, it is a social crisis.

It is not just miner against police. We live in a country where miner is
set against miner, miner against steelworker, steelworker against docker,
docker against lorry driver.

There is a general breakdown in law and order, confirmed by the
Government's own crime figures. This is in part a consequence of high
unemployment and enforced idleness among a growing section of our
population. Another side effect of the same social stress is the increased
use of sedative drugs in the NHS. Yet another is the 50% increase in
juvenile illegal drug abuse in one year and the doubling in the number of
registered drug addicts in Britain since this Government came to power.

The welfare state itself is cracking as it tries to cope with demands and
numbers its founders never foresaw. We have ripped the heart out of
whole towns and cities with thoughtless planning and brutal architecture.
We have become an altogether more aggressive society. A recent report
has marked this trend even among primary school children. They have
been brought up on a diet of routine violence on television, with video
shops peddling even more horrendous nasties.

It may be argued that since this Government has altered the balance of
advantage between rich and poor in favour of the rich, then at least there
should be one section of society which is content. But have even the rich
really benefited? Can their quality of life be said to have improved when,
during the period of this Government, the chances of their houses being
broken into have increased by 48%, the likelihood of their cars being
broken into increased by 52%, the risk of their teenagers getting hooked
on heroin has doubled? But what can you expect when there seems no
place in this harsh society for so many of our young people.

Britain is a country which has lost its way. We're a country where each
interest group or family has been encouraged to concentrate on painting
the walls of its own cabin as the ship of state founders.

That is the Britain of 1984.

It is appalling, but not yet beyond hope — if we have a sufficient
commitment to changing it.

The Prime Minister repeatedly declares her commitment to change —
of a sort. But one of the fundamental failures of this Government is that it
does not see the real extent of the problems we face, or of the obstacles to
change. There's a horrifying reek of complacency and self-satisfaction in

the face of despair and decay. How else could you describe Nigel Lawson's claim in the last major Commons debate before the summer recess that Britain has benefited from "four years of non-inflationary recovery"? If that's how they define recovery I'd like to know what they imagine decline is like.

But it's more than complacency which affects this Government; it's ignorance as well: ignorance about whole sections of British society. The most revealing sentence uttered by any minister this year was by Patrick Jenkin on visiting slums in Liverpool: "I had no idea people in Britain were living like this." Why not? What a disgraceful statement from the cabinet minister in charge of housing.

We shouldn't really be surprised. Mrs Thatcher has told us all along that she believed in a kind of social darwinism. Survival of the fittest. Government can't do everything, we are constantly told, so it should settle for taking care of the strong and hope that financial ambition and charity will do the rest. Make the rich richer and what falls from their table will be enough for the rest of us.

We too believe in encouraging the talented. But that is not the same as the survival of the fittest — the law of the jungle. Civilised government has a higher purpose — to fill the gaps left by chance or misfortune. We believe as Liberals that a society like ours must find work for all who can do it, shelter for the homeless, care for the elderly and infirm, and hope for the despairing.

There *is* despair in the eyes of millions whom Mrs Thatcher and her ministers never see. Not just the people in damp and overcrowded homes. The young couples who struggle to pay their higher mortgages; the students turned away from college or university; the elderly afraid to turn on the heating; above all despair is in the eyes of the one and a quarter million long-term unemployed.

Of the plight of all these people Tory ministers seem determinedly ignorant. The attitude of Mrs Thatcher and her colleagues towards large sections of the British people can best be described in a phrase historians used of the regard in which the citizens of ancient Rome were held by some of their less desirable emperors: "oderint dum metuant", 'let them hate me, so long as they fear me.'

There are plenty who have good reason to hate and fear her in a Britain whose enviable record of tolerance she has so successfully destroyed.

It is not just the competence of this Government which I question. It is their whole sense of values, the direction in which they want to take Britain.

Mrs Thatcher gave an interview a few weeks ago when she said of our desperate situation in Britain "I do not know any other way". What a confession. And what a contrast with that great statesman Franklin Roosevelt, who, faced by the Depression of fifty years ago and adopting

Lloyd George's ideas said "We will try something, and if it works we will keep it. If it doesn't let's try something else."

Mrs Thatcher's version of that would be "If it doesn't work, let's keep it and whatever happens let's never try anything else." Unhappily I believe the Prime Minister. She *doesn't* know any other way. Had she been a pharaoh in Egypt the slaves would not only have been ordered to make bricks without straw but to pay for the mud as well.

Yes, Prime Minister. We know your way all too well. It is a way of division, of bitterness, and, in the end, of defeat for Britain.

During the mining dispute we have seen the Thatcher way at its very worst. She appointed as Chairman of the National Coal Board an elderly American company-doctor whose reputation at British Steel had been made by cutting back rather than building up. She has effectively torn up the Plan for Coal and replaced it with nothing except a general sense of hostility to what is one of this country's major assets. She has set up a confrontation which suits her Marxist opponent Arthur Scargill very well. She has allowed attitudes to harden on both sides.

Then this week she has the nerve to talk about the strike going on for a year and demands 'victory' over the 'enemy'. It may be the Thatcher way but it is not the way to conduct industrial relations — and it is deeply damaging to the national economy.

There *is* a better way. I want to use this occasion to make a firm proposal to break the deadlock. It has three elements and it will require the recall of Parliament next week, which is perfectly possible since there are no party conferences.

The first element is that Mr MacGregor should step down immediately. He is now an impediment to a settlement. His replacement should be someone like Eric Varley who has the personal skills and the knowledge of the coal industry. The fact that he is not "one of hers" is a positive advantage. A new Chairman of the NCB is the first pre-requisite to break the log-jam.

The second element is the establishment of a new Community Rehabilitation Programme, funded by the Government. It should undertake the environmental restoration of run down mining communities to create worthwhile jobs for former miners and to get the local neighbourhood thriving again. This Programme would be loosely modelled on the excellent Villiers scheme in British Steel but will concentrate particularly on the physical environment.

This scheme should be jointly managed by the NCB and the NUM but there is one big IF. There must be a ballot on the coal strike. The Alliance will put a short Bill to the House of Commons allowing 10% of miners to trigger a national ballot. This trigger will be pointed at the head of Mr Scargill and his dictatorial ways. As the Yorkshire working miners' letter said "he is only a servant of the union". We must enable them to tell *him* what to do rather than the other way round.

I call on the Government and the TUC to out all their weight behind this scheme to set the coal industry on a new course. It is their duty to save the adversaries from themselves.

The obstacles to change in Britain are considerable. We will not carry through the changes the country needs unless we can carry the country with us.

You cannot bludgeon Britain into accepting change. That way provokes embittered resistance or nervous protectionism. The democratic way is to win change through consent. That requires a different sort of political leadership, open to ideas, quick to learn and sensitive always to the human dimensions of decisions. That is not what we have had in Britain. Successive governments have failed in the most basic political skill of all, persuasion. They bully, and sometimes they bribe, but they do not take the whole country into their confidence, do not provide a long-term sense of direction.

Unless there is a general sense of fairness, of social justice, a sense that we are all in it together, the delicate process of managing change will come unstuck. That means reconciling the necessities of industrial modernisation and technological innovation with the human needs of understanding and security. That requires democratic leadership, not authoritarian hectoring.

What leadership is the country offered?

We all know what divides Mrs Thatcher and Mr Kinnock, Tory and Labour. They tell us often enough. But since Britain's steady decline has continued under Tory and Labour governments perhaps we should also look at what unites them. That could be an important clue to what has gone wrong.

Both their Parties have come to represent the triumph of ideology over humanity and commonsense. Of course we need leadership with a strong sense of values and a clear sense of direction, but that is different from rigid ideological politics. I believe we have had it up to our necks with ideology in Britain, whether it is the half-baked marxism of the left or the fanatical market-ism of the right. It is the enemy of change by consent — and unfortunately it has now taken over both the old parties.

They both also stand for a class struggle which most sensible people hoped had been finally put to sleep in Britain after the second world war. But no, the class war is alive and prospering in the Tory and Labour Parties. It is no coincidence. Their electoral prospects depend on keeping it alive. They are united in wanting to keep the nation divided.

A third point of resemblance. They are both the loyal agents of special interests, big business for the Tories and the unions for Labour. Ask yourself why the City has done so well out of the Tories; with Lloyds protected from scandal; the Stock Exchange profitably re-shuffled at the expense of the private investor; and a rich stream of privatisation deals, crowding out more worthwhile investment in new industry.

I suggest unequivocally that it is for the same shameful reason that the Labour Government of 1974 bent over backwards in its first two years to make life easier for the unions. It is because they both have to keep their paymasters happy. For both of them the old adage is true: "whose bread I eat, whose song I sing".

But the country as a whole pays for these insider deals — and the price Britain has paid for this ideological class-based sectional leadership is immense. The special interests get looked after — but too often it has been at the expense of the public interest.

There is another way of describing the public interest which I have always liked: "the common weal", the common good. That is what has been allowed to languish and decay while the sectional interests have grown fat.

Yet we desperately need to re-create the sense of the public interest. We shall need new leadership which instead of acting for its clients, like the Tory and Labour Parties, speaks for the country as a whole — a partnership between all our citizens working together for the common weal.

You know, Mrs Thatcher and Mr Kinnock like to talk about "our people". We all know who they mean. "Our supporters, our friends, our class, our backers." I can promise you that if you ever hear me or David Owen talking about "our people" we shall mean something very different. We will mean the British people: poor *and* prosperous, North *and* South, worker *and* manager, black *and* white, men *and* women, young *and* old; *all* of the people.

For only the public interest is strong enough to restrain the vested interests. Mr Gladstone said it one hundred years ago: "All the world over I will back the masses against the classes."

The rock on which the public interest stands is our constitution, the only protection of our ancient liberties against the arbitrary power of the State.

Alone among democratic countries Britain has an unwritten constitution. It rests upon a number of assumptions, the first of which is that those who hold power will not abuse their authority.

The second is that Parliament is sovereign and government accountable to it.

The third is that the civil service owe their ultimate loyalty to the Crown, not simply to the government of the day.

The fourth is that civil liberties are sufficiently safeguarded by Parliament and by an independent judiciary.

The fifth is that public education to inform the citizen is adequately provided by a free press.

The sixth is that government itself will remain limited; that the balance between the state and the individual, between the public and private sector, between central and local government, will not be overthrown.

All these assumptions are now in jeopardy. The government's contempt for the principle of Parliamentary sovereignty is becoming more and more clear in its refusal to give adequate or accurate information on crucial questions either to the House of Commons or to its committees. Indeed, as we have seen over the Belgrano incident, ministers are prepared to engage in active misinformation to Parliament.

As I hear each new twist of government justification on that matter I cannot improve on the words Mr Asquith used of the War Office during the First World War: "They kept three sets of figures: one to mislead the public, one to mislead the Cabinet, and one to mislead themselves".

The civil service over the past five years has been bruised and battered by a government which puts loyalty above objectivity and competence. The cry "Is he one of us" shows the same attitude which led to the disastrous blunder of GCHQ.

Whether it is bans on Trade Union membership or the abuse of the Official Secrets Act — there is a systematic and despicable attempt to intimidate public servants which, when it is coupled with repeated instances of misleading Parliament, is pushing us towards an authoritarian state.

Liberals have never been satisfied that Britain's existing law and judicial system provides sufficient protection for the individual against the state. The accumulation of information in the hands of the state's agencies, as computer networks and files are centralised, provides a new threat; against which the Government has so far offered only the weakest of safeguards.

What of our free press? Well, it's not all that free. Millions are being offered in circulation-boosting competitions; tens of millions pass hands as newspapers are bought and sold, without any reference to the balance of opinion or of free expression in an increasingly Conservative national press; it is money that counts, not freedom or democracy.

On the face of it, television should be able to present a more balanced view. But in a sombre lecture given to the Edinburgh Television Festival earlier this year, Sir Denis Forman, Chairman of Granada TV, warned of "the pressures that come filtering down from most employers in ITV — and even more within the BBC — to reflect the government view".

He added that "The protection of government information has become indiscriminating and obsessional, the motive not so much to protect the security of the state as the political comfort of ministers".

Democratic institutions do not exist to make ministers comfortable. That is why in this session I re-introduced the Freedom of Information Bill.

But it is what the government is doing to local government which is perhaps the most worrying of all. Here is a Tory Party which used to be firmly committed to the principle of limited government now pushing into effect the most massive centralisation of power in the hands of the executive.

If a *Labour* government was introducing rate-capping and replacing the metropolitan councils with a new collection of nominated bodies under ministerial control, Conservative rhetoric would flow; it would be, correctly, attacked as state socialism, imposing on every town and village in Britain the rule that the men in Whitehall know best.

Here is a government which set out to redeem Mrs Thatcher's pledge to abolish rates, which is instead stumbling blindly towards the virtual abolition of local democracy.

And now if the documents leaked to us at the start of the week are correct they are turning their guns in precisely the same way on the administration of the nationalised industries.

The virtue of an unwritten constitution, it used to be said, is that it is flexible. But if the flexible conventions on which our democracy rests are bent too far, they will break.

There is one further constitutional safeguard we will introduce — repeal of the 1981 Nationality Act. Some of the strongest opposition to the Act came from the leaders of the Churches who unequivocally condemned it. In February the General Synod of the Church of England passed a motion pressing for substantial changes in the Act which members described as "racist, unfair, divisive and repugnant to the Christian conscience". That well known pillar of the Synod Mr John Gummer prudently decided to stay away — so much for the Christian principles which he so ostentatiously parades at the slightest provocation — or even without it.

The Act gives enormous discretion and huge powers to the Home Secretary. Fine if you are a prosperous and Christian family living in a Tory village in a country where a by-election is pending; the Home Secretary will then be graciously pleased to listen to all the representations which have been made and allow you to stay. I was delighted for Mr and Mrs Pereira, but equally I am appalled to consider what happened to an unemployed Bangladeshi woman, Afia Begum, who with her child born here, was ruthlessly deported, only because her husband died before she could be registered. And there are far, far too many similar cases of hardship inflicted on innocent people because of a vicious circle of oppression. We enact unjust racist laws, the poor and the powerless are trapped by them, and then when they appeal against them, we wash our hands, and piously declaim that the law must be obeyed.

Those individual cases, and they are countless, which the Home Secretary so callously dismisses, are suffering human beings, victims of the inhuman laws which he so ruthlessly administers. And now, in a new departure from former practice, even MPs are not to be allowed to raise questions of immigration appeals, except in their own constituencies, and the whole tenor of Home Office attitudes is that all representations will now be considered counter-productive.

This is doubly shameful for the Home Secretary; for he comes from a community which has known horrendous persecution and racial discrimination down the centuries — on this issue, at least, one might have hoped that a sense of humanity would triumph over conservative prejudice.

So constitutional reform must be a central issue in the Alliance campaign. We aim to open up British government, to force ministers to justify themselves and their proposals before the public. We aim to give Parliament effective control over the executive. We aim to free the civil service from the covert pressures of executive secrecy, and to redraw the boundary between political advice and administrative discretion.

We will introduce a Bill of Rights, to protect the citizen against the state; and we may need to reform the structure of the legal professional and judiciary. We will revitalise local democracy, cutting away at the spreading tentacles of nominated bodies and local and regional decisions to democratic control. And we will, of course, give Britain what every other democratic country in Europe already has: a representative electoral system.

The Thatcher economic experiment has failed. Look at the evidence: investment down. The economic indicators pointing down, manufactured trade in deficit, and unemployment inexorably creeping up. No wonder the pound is sliding to an all-time low, unable to resist the challenge of a strong dollar. No wonder that the flow of private capital out of Britain has become a flood.

You know the economic recovery we were promised, the recovery that would make all the hardship worthwhile. Well, we just had it — and most people didn't even notice.

A change is of course essential. North Sea oil production is at peak. As it runs down, our economy will be exposed in all its weakness.

Of course competition has its place. But the blind gods of the market place alone are not going to show us the way out of this industrial crisis.

The only possible way forward is the Liberal way. It is actually to treat the talented people of this country as the precious resource they are, and to liberate their energy and enthusiasm to work together to rebuild a derelict economy.

How do you do that? You do it by changing the tax system, tackling the poverty trap, reducing national insurance charges to encourage employers to take people on, especially the young and the long-term unemployed.

You do it by educating and training people, developing and renewing each person's skills, as the Germans already do and the new French Prime Minister plans to do.

You do it by a total government commitment to the new technology, with special education centres and training, tax incentives and credit-free loans for companies switching over to British technology.

You do it by an incomes strategy which ends the Conservative policy of taking money from the wage-earner and handing it to the rich, and substitute a sense of fairness in which everyone shares in success rather than scrambling for paper wage increases. You relate that strategy to the greatest possible extension of shared profit and shared ownership, and the smaller units of the new industries are the ideal spawning ground for shared control and ownership.

You build a partnership of private and public capital through regional development agencies and local enterprise initiatives. That will fertilise the economy at the grass roots, creating new companies and new jobs.

You ensure that the government, on its own account and through nationalised industries, buys and invests in Britain — and you persuade large British companies to do the same, encouraging and developing a multitude of smaller companies who supply them. Like Marks & Spencer, each large company should recognise its responsibility for developing British supplies and raising their standards.

Basically what you do — and what an Alliance Government *will* do — is to make people partners in a common enterprise. Partners in changing *their* lives, *their* neighbourhoods, *their* workplaces, and in the end *their* country. We need a new industrial revolution in Britain, but it won't happen without a profound change in attitudes. That means putting people first. Then we shall have a successful revolution by consent.

For it is our aim to form an Alliance Government. And that *is* a realistic aim. We should not underestimate the strength of the foundations we have already built.

The tide is more than ever running our way. In the six by-elections of this year, we have won one, and come within a whisker of two more. In these contests, almost 37% supported the Alliance — only 32% the Conservative Government and even less — 29% — the official Labour opposition.

The Gallup Poll ratings have averaged 22% throughout that period — again, an unusually good indicator of our underlying strength, and broadly reflecting our performance in the European elections. Last week's Gallup Poll put our rating at 25.5% — back to our strength in the General Election.

And of course our force in local government grows daily. At the beginning of the last decade, Liberals had only begun to break into the municipal strongholds of Tory and Labour.

But it is in *this* decade that we have moved on — holding and sharing power in an increasing number of Town Halls. The two-party system may hang on in Westminster — but locally, it's being knocked to pieces. And only this last Thursday, Liberals won an astonishing 12 seats in local council by-elections. No wonder we look with confidence to the County Council elections next year.

Our electoral base is therefore strong — and growing. We are vastly more experienced and hardheaded — in our campaigning and in our determination to achieve victory.

What this Assembly signals is nothing less than the start of a three year election campaign, not a three week one, to offer our people an alternative government. In a real sense the Labour Party has become an obstacle in the way of defeating the Conservative government. They may still be the official opposition. But we are the effective opposition. Because no-one can take seriously a party so deeply divided on every major issue. I do not blame Mr Kinnock personally. He, like Michael Foot before him, is trying to do a hopeless job. They cannot reconcile the irreconcilable.

The loony left are taking over in the constituencies, in the council chambers, in some of the unions and already among the back benchers of the Commons.

They are already stuck with a new programme less acceptable than the last. Nationalisation without compensation and an economic policy described by Roy Hattersley during his quest for leadership as "literally incredible".

Our task in the Alliance is to finish the job we began at the last election of elbowing Labour out of the way and going for Government in 1987 or 1988. Of course if we don't achieve that we may have to use our second or substantial third place to secure both electoral reform and stable reforming government. We must in that event declare our readiness to work with others for these objectives.

But make no mistake, our *purpose* must be to offer the British people at the next election a choice of government which will take us in a major reforming direction. That was a primary objective in forming our alliance with the SDP. We must have no lesser aim.

When I say that, the Tories sometimes say, "that's all very well, but who have you got?"

Who have we got? What a nerve! What is it they think we cannot match?

The judgement of Patrick Jenkin?

The humanity and charm of Norman Tebbit?

The modesty of Michael Heseltine?

The charisma of Geoffrey Howe?

The down to earth common sense of Keith Joseph?

Or is it the sheer weight of John Selwyn Gummer?

Perhaps it is just the sharp shooting of Willie Whitelaw?

I tell you this, the Iron Lady's team is in fact no match at all for that of the Steel Man.

I lead a team of highly talented young MPs and of experienced peers. Together with the formidable ministerial record of many in the SDP and the wealth of talent among the candidates of both parties I have absolute confidence that we would provide as fresh and able a government as took power in 1906 after nine years of Conservative rule.

Who would have though five years ago that we would have taking part in our Assembly a former Chairman of the National Coal Board, a former Chancellor of the Exchequer and a former Chief of the Defence Staff. Who would have thought that we would have grown from 1,000 to 2,000 councillors.

We have developed a maturity that allows us to face the challenge of entering government — and the difficult negotiations that go with it — with great confidence. We now have less than three years to prepare for that decisive test. The dramatic victory at Portsmouth South illustrated the potency of a united and integrated Alliance.

The Alliance has continued to grow together since last year's general election. And campaigning together, we will grow yet closer.

Our first priority in the year ahead is to build up our membership and strengthen our local and national organisation. Next week you will be out on the doorstep, seeking out new members in a determined drive. Work at it. We know the potential is there. It is vital to our challenge.

Our second priority is to get a complete slate of first-class parliamentary candidates into the field. Candidate selection must be settled amicably and quickly. Every month that passes shortens the time which we have to prepare for the coming fight.

Our third priority lies in refining our policy. Abiding by the unchanging principles of Liberalism — yet developing new ideas to meet the challenge of the 1990s.

I have a message for every Liberal and Social Democrat throughout the country. You represent the only hope of saving Britain from the disaster of a third-term Thatcher Government.

If we are to succeed over the next three years we will have to surrender small parts of our individual interests, to build a platform we can all stand on, comfortably, proudly, singing out the truth for the nation to hear, its message so clear and commanding, that no slick advertising campaign, no amount of press bias, no amount of unfair broadcasting coverage, will be able to muffle it.

I want to make a special appeal to the young to come in and join us in this three year crusade.

The policies of this Government and their political allies the Reaganites have not made this world a safer or a better place.

They have done nothing to solve the problems of the Middle East which as I saw for myself again last week remains a highly dangerous flashpoint of world tension. With their money and political support they have in many parts of the world backed the wrong people. It is not Communism that is the enemy in Latin America it is injustice and poverty.

We have totally lacked in Britain in these last years any real commitment to our friends or to our ideals, or any consistent priority for basic human rights. We Liberals champion equally the Refusniks and the Sakharovs, the Bishop Tutus and Nelson Mandelas struggling for freedom in South Africa.

And how long can we go on turning our backs as this Government has done on the international responsibilities imposed on us by our own history, our own wealth and the crying needs of others.

I spoke at the outset of the sort of country we want Britain to be. A country is not strong because of the size of its armies and it is not powerful because of its world wide investments. A country today can be influential in the world by the size of its heart and the breadth of its mind, and that is the role I want for Britain. We must give the lead in ending the condition described in Housman's lines where:

"Envious of heart, blind-eyed, with tongues confounded
Nation by nation still goes unforgiven
In wrath and fear by jealousies surrounded,
Building proud towers which shall not reach to heaven."

This country itself is not like a grey blanket, a piece of unbroken cloth, the same colour and texture throughout. I see it more as a quilt, many patches, many pieces, many shapes, all woven and held together by a common thread. The white, the black, the industrialist, the trade unionist, the small businessman, the farmer, the unemployed, the peace campaigner, the disabled, the mentally handicapped. Even in our fractured state all of us count and all of us fit in somewhere.

When I was at university there was a particularly odious but short-lived student society called P.L.U. — People Like Us — which existed to wear certain old school ties and scarves. In their very different ways the Conservative and Labour parties exist only for people like themselves.

A society which as they do emphasises uniformity is one which creates intolerance and hate. They want others to conform to their view of how we should live. Our standard in all activities should be one of excellence, but our routes to its achievement may be as numerous as there are Britons who pursue it.

In a true sense, neither the Conservative nor Labour Parties can any longer claim to be national parties. There are admittedly still some places where our Alliance parties are not thick on the ground. But look at the Tory Party; in the great industrial cities of Glasgow and Liverpool they have no longer a single MP. You will search the entire country south of the line from London to Bristol and not find a single Labour MP. Yet we are building everywhere.

One of the great figures of my constituency, John Buchan, wrote of early seventeenth century Britain that: "the old world was crumbling and there was no unanimity about the new". Britain today needs to decide whether to stand still with the past or move forward. And at the moment we simply lack the national leadership capable of creating a coherent framework of "unanimity about the new". How can they, when the very raison d'etre of the Tory and Labour parties is against the search for consensus or unanimity?

Unlike these parties, we genuinely embrace men and women of every condition, of every economic class, or every creed, of every orientation, in every part of the country. In our family are gathered everyone from the abject poor in the slums of our great cities to the enlightened well-to-do in the suburbs. White collar and blue collar, young professional, the teenaged unemployed. They're all there.

We are proud of this diversity which you won't find next month in the Labour and Tory conferences. The different people we represent have many points of view. We have debates, even arguments. Some criticise us for it, but it is part of our strength.

At the end we are stronger for having listened to each other. If we need any inspiration to set aside our small differences all we need do is reflect on the Tory policy of divide and rule to see how grievously it has injured our land.

I spoke earlier of our commitment to the public interest against special interest. We have an obligation to each other to build a finer democracy, one in which our fellow citizens have the chance to work, to make the world better for their children and to be protected in these moments when they would not be able to protect themselves.

The young of this generation must exercise the right to dream. You must face the reality that is, but then dream of the reality that ought to be, that must be. Live beyond the pain of reality with that dream of a bright tomorrow.

Use hope and imagination as tools for survival and progress.

I see a Britain in our time where greed, self-interest and division are vanquished by the common good, and the national interest.

We believe that government should be a positive force to solve problems, and that public service is a worthwhile vocation.

We believe in only the government we need but we insist on all the government we need.

Our bold strategies are rooted in our basic Liberal values and we have the courage to carry them out. What is called for is an exercise in government at its best.

We believe in government of fairness and reason, a government that doesn't promise to do what it cannot do.

A government strong enough to use the words "love" and "compassion" and capable of converting our hopes and dreams into practical reality.

If you share our vision of what Britain could be, come with us on this three year haul.

It will happen if we make it happen, and we are determined to make it happen.

1985

At the Dundee Liberal Assembly.

Chapter Ten

The turn of the tide

David Steel made two speeches at the 1984 Liberal Assembly at Bournemouth. One had been his usual 'tour de force' on the Friday afternoon, effectively concluding the Conference. But the other was an altogether more spontaneous contribution, delivered earlier in the week during the defence debate.

Liberal Party delegates in the Assembly's Commission on Defence and Disarmament, had that year deliberated and agonised for most of the week over a portmanteau of a draft resolution.

Entitled, "Uniting for Peace", it did almost that, stretching over most of the cracks between the unilateral nuclear disarmers and the unrepentant supporters of Western collective security and the NATO nuclear umbrella.

One crucial difference remained, however, and that was over the thorny issue of cruise missiles. Back in 1981, the Liberal Assembly had delivered a rebuff to the leadership by voting decisively against an acceptance by Britain of cruise missiles on British soil. Such a rejection was unconditional — whereas David Steel had wanted to see their deployment or otherwise linked to success at the negotiating table — and had raised the spectre that the Liberal Party was "going unilateral".

In the event, Alliance MPs had voted in Parliament against approving the deployment of cruise missiles, expressing the view that insufficient progress had been made by the United States at the INF negotiations in Geneva to justify a further escalation in the nuclear arms race.

Three years after the Llandudno vote, the Assembly once again considered cruise missiles. This time the question was not their deployment, but their removal. Should this be immediate or unconditional, or could it merely be as part of a negotiated settlement? The Chairman of the Defence Commission, and the man who had been given the task of pulling the Party together on the defence issue, was Paddy Ashdown. The original mover of the 1981 Assembly resolution, he had since been elected Liberal MP for Yeovil, and therefore had influence over both wings of the Party. Perhaps he had the authority to fashion a compromise, namely: support for a nuclear "freeze" to stop further deployment, but leaving those cruise missiles already in place to be removed by negotiation.

It was not to be. Whatever his motivation, Ashdown finally decided to step aside from his healing role and instead urged the Assembly as before to reject cruise missiles lock stock and barrel.

Against all the advice, David Steel decided to attempt to dissuade the Assembly from taking a course which he knew would be misinterpreted and which would make life with David Owen and the SDP immeasurably more difficult. In an act of great courage, David Steel left the platform and took the debate onto the Conference floor.

The tide of opinion proved too strong. Few in the Party seemed to appreciate that the strength of feeling against cruise did not represent a dangerous lurch towards unilateral disarmament (although many delgates supported that view) but represented a genuine distaste for what was seen as a particularly dangerous and inappropriate new weapons system.

Steel lost the vote, but his reputation soared. In one short speech he had provided the answer to those who doubted his courage or his strength of purpose.

Electorally, matters were also starting to improve. Between June and December 1984, the opinion polls had put Alliance support at between 21-23%. Between January and May 1985, there was a modest but steady growth in support. A quarter of the electorate now regularly admitted to backing the Alliance and in May that support jumped to 29%.

More important than any opinion poll, however, were the County Council election results on May 1st. Results from 47 English and Welsh Counties not only showed a big swing to the Alliance (with 304 seats being gained) but there was a tangible increase in real Alliance influence. Not only did the Alliance (through the Liberals) comfortably retain control of the Isle of Wight, but no fewer than 21 Shire Counties ended election night as 'hung' Councils — or with "life in the balance", as the Liberals preferred to call it — with Alliance Councillors exercising real power.

Whatever the outward appearance might have been, the two-party system was breaking up fast on the ground as multi-party politics became a reality.

Further good news came in June, in the Brecon and Radnor by-election. In a closely fought contest, which Labour had been widely expected to win, Richard Livsey, for the Alliance, narrowly took the seat by 559 votes, becoming the eighteenth Liberal Member of Parliament, and the 25th Alliance MP.

In the Autumn, the Liberal Party held its Annual Assembly in the solid Scottish City of Dundee, on the banks of the Tay.

David Steel approached his Assembly speech in a confident mood.

The Labour Party, despite its new Leader and a great deal of public relations froth, had not managed to shake loose its image as a Party still anxious to hide its unacceptable Militant face from the electorate.

The "Thatcher Revolution" continued — but against targets which were arousing the hostility and opposition of those who in the past had been among the Conservative Party's most loyal and traditional supporters.

David Steel himself was back in business — now over half-way through the Parliamentary term — and beginning to detect the scent of the coming battle in his nostrils.

Electorally, the Alliance was on the move. The next election would present them with a vital opportunity.

Would this be "The turn of the tide"?

> The whistle has blown for kick-off in the second half of this parliament. By half-time we had built up a good score. We must keep our nerve as the government team starts to use rougher and dirtier tactics in the second half.
>
> They have good reason to be afraid. We are playing up-field. We surged forward in the county council elections in May. In large parts of Britain Alliance councillors are giving people the experience of a new sort of open and effective local government.
>
> Since May, in local by-elections across the whole country, voters have given victory after famous victory to Liberals and our SDP allies.
>
> And not just at the expense of the Tories. We have been making inroads

into Labour heartlands such as the Nottingham coalfields and Inner London.

In fact, our lead has been widening. You don't have to bank on the opinion polls. If you add up all the votes cast in council by-elections over the last three months we have polled 37%, Labour 32% and the Conservatives only 29%. Here in Scotland we have reduced Labour control in Aberdeen to a knife-edge and across the silvery Tay we control North East Fife District Council.

Our steady march forward in *local* government has been matched by the great *parliamentary* triumph of Brecon and Radnor. But as we have seen so vividly in these last two weeks Brecon was no isolated beacon of hope.

It's not surprising that the other parties feel threatened by our success. Last week I warned the SDP to expect a furious campaign of misrepresentation by the Tories and their tame Press lords. It has already started.

It is obviously going to be noisy and squalid. So I wonder if, in the public interest, I might make a sort of political Noise Abatement proposal to the new Tory Party Chairman: "Norman, if you stop telling lies about us, we'll stop telling the truth about you."

Incidentally I notice Norman Tebbit has acquired a new assistant, Mr Jeffrey Archer, who, I am told by Debbie Owen, writes books. A novel appointment. Looking at them together, I found myself thinking of the old axiom that truth is stranger than fiction.

Internally we have made good progress too: together with our SDP partners we have reached agreement in almost 600 of the parliamentary seats and many candidates are already chosen and campaigning.

My message to them is this: you are our "MPs-in-waiting". You have the support of a team of regional organisers, of a newly-formed campaign unit in Parliament and of the joint policy programme "Priorities for the Nineties" which the Alliance will publish in 1986. We shall also have a streamlined Party Headquarters in a new suite of offices in the National Liberal Club. Sadly the man who has done so much to build this electoral fighting machine, John Spiller, has had to retire through ill-health. John, we thank you and hope you will be fit enough to join us at the next election. That's one that nobody should miss.

When that election comes, the Alliance will be the only credible alternative to Thatcherism. We are established everywhere and growing everywhere. By contrast Labour is a party in retreat, driven back to its traditional class and regional fortresses.

I don't propose to waste the time of this Assembly by dwelling on the so-called Official Opposition. Yet spare just one thought for poor Mr Kinnock, leading a party in long-term decline. He has accused me of putting the hype into hypothetical. Posing as an alternative Prime Minister he has certainly put the babble into the impro-bable. I say poor

Mr Kinnock because the leadership of the Labour Party has become a position of responsibility without power.

The power belongs to the trade union paymasters, like Ron Todd, Ken Gill and Arthur Scargill, and to the town-hall militants like Ted Knight in London, Derek Hatton in Liverpool and Alex Wood in Edinburgh. They, for their part, have no sense of responsibility to anyone, certainly not their members or electors. Power is all they care about. But let me tell you this. Come the election the British people will refuse both responsibility *and* power to Labour's warring factions — and they will be right to do so.

So we must very seriously prepare ourselves for government — and incidentally, I wouldn't say that Liberals are not ready for government. It is government that isn't ready for the Liberals. Whitehall is going to have to come to terms with a different way of working — from a reforming Alliance, with a more open style.

But preparing for government is not just a matter of having effective administrative machinery and the right policies. I want today to concentrate on the values and attitudes which make good government possible in a complicated modern democracy like ours. The values and attitudes of this government are plain wrong, which is why their policies are wrong and why they cannot succeed in introducing many of the changes which are needed. The old politics are running out of steam because they are running out of consent.

Good government works with the grain, not against the grain. That is the trouble with Thatcherism — it goes against the grain.

You sometimes get the feeling that the Prime Minister's definition of the enemy within has been expanded to include most of the British people. We are all 'moaning minnies' now. Her highest ideals are the shabby values of Dallas or Dynasty, where the poor are kept safely off the screen.

In pursuit of the fast buck, Thatcherism has been prepared to leave a trail of destruction behind it, but this radicalism of the right has been strangely selective. Thatcherism hasn't tackled the real obstacles to progress — the professional closed shops, the lucrative old boy deals in the City, the excessive overtime that puts people out of work, the cover-ups in Whitehall, the inefficiency in Parliament or the concentration of half the nation's wealth into the hands of the few.

No, the target of the new wreckers of the right has been the wealth of institutions that embody the basic British values of fairness and tolerance; institutions which are admired abroad as at home, and which best express what I call the British genius, that makes our country special. Just look at a few examples.

Take the BBC. Now, Aunty BBC is by no means perfect but nevertheless we all have reason to be grateful for its existence. It is a strong and respected pillar of democracy in Britain, admired and envied in other countries throughout the world.

Yet this government, irritated by the independence of the BBC, has set out to commercialise it, to control it and to dismember it. Friends of democratic pluralism should be friends of the BBC, determined to defend it from the Prime Minister and her philistine friends.

Aunty is our guarantee that Nanny does not get things all her own way.

Take another manifestation of the British genius, the scientific research on which our future depends.

In this century British scientists have won more Nobel Prizes than any country except the USA. Our scientists command immense international respect.

Yet through indiscriminate cost-cutting, the Government has been attacking them and their prospects in a way which makes me tremble for our commercial future. Laboratories are closing, entire research units are being disbanded and vital equipment is not being purchased.

The Medical Research Council, the Agricultural Research Council, the Natural Environment Research Council and the Scientific and Engineering Council are all under pressure.

You can see the results. The overseas brain-drain of able young scientists is accelerating. Unfortunately this is part of a wider pattern of neglect of higher education of all kinds. The contraction of universities and colleges at the very time when we should be investing in our future flies in the face of common sense.

A further expression of the British genius has been our history of local democracy.

We ought to be building on that tradition. Our people should have, and wish to have, more say in the decisions affecting their lives. The process of government has become too complex. We aim to simplify it.

To that end, within two years of winning the General Election, we are determined to introduce the legislation needed to provide for the setting up of Scottish and Welsh Parliaments — assemblies fashioned to meet the distinct needs and aspirations of their respective nations, and with local government streamlined in both countries into a single tier of effective, multi-purpose authorities, close to the people.

That pattern of decentralisation, once established in a legislative framework, will also allow us to shift power to the people and regions of England as the demand takes shape.

The dead hand of centralisation must be resisted wherever this Tory government extends its grip; not only here in Scotland but increasingly over local authorities throughout Britain; for the Alderman's daughter has attacked the very principle of local government itself.

Liberals have long been critics of both the GLC and the metropolitan counties. But we have never been attracted to the idea of tearing down without putting something better in its place.

Moreover, a mixture of political prejudice and administrative frustration cannot justify her unconstitutional abolition of elected authorities without consent.

Abolition, ratecapping, financial penalties, the remorseless reduction in rate support grant, the freezing of £6,000 million capital receipts — in fact the endless stream of interference with local government does not defeat the government's political opponents. What it does is to destroy local democracy itself.

Voters turn away in cynical despair from the powerlessness of what should be their Councils; and fewer and fewer men and women of goodwill feel it is worthwhile freely giving their time and energy in the service of the local community. The genius that inspired Chamberlain's Birmingham or Morrison's London, which made the boroughs and the shires the first flowers of British democracy, is being snuffed out. Now the grey wastes of the "republic of mediocrity", in which the "woman in Whitehall" knows best, threatens to replace the local autonomy and variety which once were our pride.

Another element of what makes this country unique, is our matchless countryside — William Blake's "green and pleasant land". In the 1930s Green Belts — another example of British genius — were first introduced to stop the ruin of the land by the uncontrolled sprawling development of the towns and cities.

Yet incredibly this government is now moving in to attack the Green Belts at the behest of a consortium of building developers who want the easy profits from developing green field sites. At Hook in Hampshire earlier this year I supported those protesting at having 6,000 new houses dumped next to their village. They won that fight but now the threat is aimed at a 720 acre green field site at Tillingham Hall in Essex.

The government's own figures show that over 18,000 acres of derelict land are currently held by public authorities in the South-east alone. Certainly we need more houses but our priority should be to build them in our run-down and neglected cities, not in our precious countryside.

Another expression of the British genius has been to look outward from these islands to the world. That quality has never been more badly needed than today but under this government Britain's influence for good around the world has been dissipated. We may be only a middle-ranking power nowadays but our history and international experience give us a unique opportunity to be a force for justice, for human rights, for peace and disarmament.

The present British government has become identified with the most narrow-minded and conservative elements in the world.

In a European community, which is seeking greater political unity and completion of the internal market, the Prime Minister's contribution has been broken-bottle diplomacy, hectoring our friends and abusing her colleagues.

She has lagged behind the civilised community of nations again and again: on disarmament talks where she refuses to put Polaris on the negotiating table, frustrates the prospects for a Comprehensive Test Ban treaty and the renewal of the Non-Proliferation Treaty and pursues the blatant unilateral nuclear escalation of Trident; on Central America where the government has ranged itself consistently with the forces of reaction; on the Middle East, where she looks for what Britain can gain from the conflict, not for what we can contribute to its solution; and on South Africa where she over-rides the Foreign Office in seeing "positive aspects" in President Botha's stonewalling speech and where we now stand isolated in our refusal to support sanctions.

Martin Luther King once spoke of "the appalling silence of the good people". Because Mrs Thatcher cares more for Britain's investment in South Africa than for the basic civil rights of the majority people of that country, the good people of Britain have been silenced. Gagged by their own government.

Mrs. Thatcher mistakes the attitudes of the good British people. She thinks they share her slavish devotion to Ronald Reagan. She thinks they believe with her that everyone who opposes the tin-pot dictators and millionaire landlords of the Third World must be a communist.

Our Prime Minister under-rates the tradition of imagination and generosity in Britain towards the poor and wretched of the world. We saw it when people crammed into village and town halls to hear about the Brandt Report — and more recently when the famine in Ethiopia was shown on television it was the people who led the way. After Band-Aid, Live-Aid demonstrated that the spontaneous outburst of concern had deep and enduring roots. The good people led the way while the government found its extra aid for Ethiopia and Sudan by raiding other parts of our already reduced aid budget. The people put the government to shame.

Within twenty-five years four out of five people will live in the developing world.

If the nations of the North cannot speak to those of the South: if the international economic crisis, and the huge rise in indebtedness is not tackled imaginatively; if trade withers as protectionism and chauvinism grow, if we continue to see growing expenditure on arms in both East and West, we shall fail. There will be no world unless we find the way to one world.

The ideal of public service is central to the British spirit. Yet this government has set out to denigrate public servants and the whole public sector. The damage that has been done to the morale of the civil service is reflected in the rising numbers of men and women leaving, and in the leaks which continue to seep from disillusioned civil servants despite draconian efforts to maintain official secrecy.

I am not just talking about senior civil servants. Top people have been well looked after. It is the dedicated ordinary public servant whom we take for granted, clerical officers who struggle to deal with the mountains of government paper, customs officers trying to stem the flood of hard drugs into Britain, the social security staff who find themselves caught between their clients and an uncaring government, the inland revenue staff operating an inequitable and over-complicated tax system, the nurses, who are expected to work for love and loyalty; the teachers, under-valued by a government which cares far more about private education than public education, and by a Secretary of State who would scarcely survive for half an hour in a secondary school classroom. It isn't just the holding-down of salaries which has depressed the morale of so many of those who work for the common good or our community. It is the government's evident lack of respect for the contribution they make.

Sir Robert Armstrong, the senior civil servant in the land, himself the recipient of a 48% increase in pay, circulated a civil service memorandum last year which blurred the boundary between official loyalty to the government of the day and the wider loyalty to the crown. It's a dangerous development to suggest that officials must in all circumstances obey the instructions of their political superiors; we put people on trial in Nuremberg for doing that. And with real vindictiveness the government is still pursuing those staff at GCHQ who are right to insist that the defence of a free society must mean the defence of free trade unions.

And so at the end of eight years of Conservative government, Britain will be a poorer country in every way — less prosperous, meaner in spirit, with less to be proud of.

Yes, the rich will be richer — but this is the only respect in which the Thatcher revolution will have succeeded. The next government — and I believe it will be the Alliance next — will face the grim reality of the post oil era with a weakened economy, a more divided society and widespread pessimism about the future. The legacy we inherit will be a heavy mortgage on Britain's future.

So what will we do about it?

We must embark on a revolution of our own, a revolutionary shift in values and attitudes.

First we must re-kindle the British genius. We must junk all this monetarist and socialist ideology and get back to basics. And for any Liberal the basics are very simple — they are the potential of each individual. We must liberate all the wasted energy of the people of this country by finding new ways to work together rather than against each other. We must create a new partnership in every company, in every community and in the nation as a whole.

The role of government is not to command — as Conservatives and Socialists both believe — it is to enable: to enable each individual to use his or her talents to the full — and incidentally what sort of country is it that fails to use all the talents of half its people, its women — to enable industry and commerce to thrive; to enable the arts and learning to flourish; and to enable political decisions to be made at the level of the people most affected by them.

An enabling government, which treats each citizen as a partner, which shares its ideas instead of imposing them is going to be essential in the difficult decades ahead.

But at the same time, we need some positive new ideas from government. Who cares if we mix up socialism and capitalism a bit if we can get things moving. Let me illustrate what I mean by sketching out three proposals:

First, partnership in industry.

The key to industrial recovery in Britain does not lie in the vaults of City banks but in the capable hands of the managers and employees of our companies. There is a wealth of energy, enthusiasm and inventiveness waiting to be unlocked.

How do we turn the key? By transforming each employee from a wage-slave into a partner in his or her enterprise. As John Stuart Mill put it "by accustoming them to the comprehension of joint interests, the management of joint concerns — uniting them instead of isolating them from one another".

Partnership is an idea whose time has come, and only our partnership of the Alliance can introduce it because it threatens the whole basis of Conservative and Socialist ideology. They want a struggle between the two sides of industry. We want a successful joint concern, a share economy.

The Conservative government remains firmly opposed to legislation for employee involvement. They thought they could get away with a vague requirement for companies to report on their employee involvement policies each year.

However, a recent study of 100 company reports by the Institute of Directors has demonstrated convincingly that even this limited approach is not working. The survey found that only 9% of the companies provided any information.

I cannot help wondering why the Government is dragging its heels.

Employee involvement not only improves business efficiency, but also improves employee responsibility and job satisfaction. But we want to go further. I've spent some time in the last year visiting companies who've been a bit bolder in this field.

At Jaguar in Coventry I was impressed by the remarkable recovery the company has achieved in the last few years. The introduction of an incentive scheme, an employee share ownership scheme and improved communication, were central to their recovery plan.

At the National Freight Consortium, an organisation which spans the country, more than 82% of all shares are owned by the workforce — and two-thirds of the employees now have some stake in their company. Trading profit has more than doubled since the buy-out in 1981.

The Baxi Heating Company near Preston — one of whose works council meetings I attended last month — is even more remarkable. They have long believed in employee participation. They operate a cash profit sharing scheme and in 1983 the old family company was converted into a partnership, making Baxi the largest manufacturing group in Britain to be wholly owned by its employees. The entire workforce from top management to the shop floor have become owners. Supervision is kept to a minimum. Jobs are rotated on a regular basis. Everyone eats in the same canteen.

Independent researchers have been consistently surprised by the strength of the commitment and morale within the company. Labour/ management relations are good, job satisfaction is high and the company is successful financially.

Firms like these should be an example to us all. Employees should everywhere be treated as full partners, their contribution valued and respected and this way the trench between labour and management can be finally bridged. The CBI this morning has warned that pay rises in the private sector should be held to about 4% and they are probably right, but what about profits? They say employees are "showing an increased understanding of the need for profits". Wouldn't the employees show even more understanding, if on top of the 4%, a share of those profits was going into their pockets?

For the nation's economy profit sharing could reduce our susceptibility to wage-push inflation. Our Alliance government will insist on it as part of our comprehensive incomes strategy and so help to create jobs.

All this sounds plain common sense. But don't think you'll get industrial partnership out of a Labour government or a Conservative government. They won't do it because they can't do it.

Second, a partnership to regenerate our inner cities. If ever there was a problem which needs some new thinking it is their plight — as the events in Handsworth last week so tragically reminded us.

I have no doubt there were criminal acts and they should be dealt with by the law. But criminals alone do not produce riots. The riots in British cities which we have seen too often in recent years, whether sparked off by criminals, agitators or simply by aggressive and frustrated young men, depend on the dry stubble of despair to get the blaze really going.

My eyes were really opened this summer. I spent a week in Liverpool. I saw its sunny side and its slummy side. On the sunny side was a cellar jazz club in a renovated dockside warehouse. On the slummy side were boarded up shops and broken glass. On the sunny side was the housing co-operative in Vauxhall who invited me in to one of their developments for 200 families. On the slummy side were the semi-abandoned tower blocks. On the sunny side was the cheerful welcome of the black self-help group; on the slummy side was the devastation of hard drugs.

One drug addict I talked with put it bluntly. He said they saw no reason for giving up drugs. What was there to give up drugs for? Where was the job? Where was the hope? For them rather the unreality of drugs than the reality of the life on offer.

What is needed in our inner city areas is a ferment of new ideas. I found some on the sunny side. People working together to get things done for their own communities. And that must be our starting point. It is no good telling them to get on their bikes and go elsewhere. It is precisely the people with initiative, the self starters, who must be persuaded to stay if these communities are to thrive. Otherwise we shall be left with a permanent underclass of those who cannot escape — the single parents, the unskilled, the ethnic minorities, the elderly — eking out a frightened existence in the twilight zones.

We must make the inner cities fit places to live in, to encourage back the talented who have left and to bring in new blood. It is not the faceless concrete monuments to municipal socialism that we need; not the Eastern European style banners disfiguring the finest public buildings in Liverpool or Edinburgh or Islington; it is a programme of detailed small scale investment in renovating and brightening up run-down housing, in planting grass and trees on the waste sites, in building low cost housing that young people can afford and in incentives for the creation of thriving small businesses.

We must also give the people a stake in their communities with elected neighbourhood councils; we must bring together the police and the public in a combined effort to defeat criminals and protect the community. I believe it is the local community itself which, if democratically organised, will be the best planner for its own needs.

Most important of all, we must give people something to do. The unemployed individual becomes bored and frustrated; television brings into the home a world which is full of enticing goods and lifestyles which the unemployed cannot afford. No wonder bitterness sets in and sometimes boils over.

Our Alliance government will match the people waiting for something to do with the tasks waiting to be done.

I now turn to a wide area where the partnership approach will help us. Using new ideas to solve old problems is nowhere more relevant than in generating capital investment for our run-down economy. Make no mistake, if we win the election our chancellor will find the public expenditure cupboard is very bare indeed. Government borrowing will worsen by the £3 to £4 billion per year of privatisation asset sales no longer available. Nigel Lawson is currently cooking the books by calling these reduced spending. In Richard Wainwright's memorable phrase he has been selling the furniture to pay the housekeeping bills.

The massive oil revenues, worth nearly £13 billion during the Thatcher years and so tragically frittered away, will be falling fast.

The strains on the Public Sector Borrowing Requirement will be immense. The Alliance must not over-promise.

As we showed in our excellent economic motion yesterday, we do not propose to solve our economic problems by massive commitments to extra public spending.

We must find ways to use public funds to unlock private investment. There is a wealth of private investment money, both here and from abroad, looking for a secure return. Socialists turn up their noses at private investment and Tories, as we have seen, are opposed to public investment on equally doctrinaire grounds.

What the Alliance must do is to discard these shibboleths and initiate a new partnership between public and private investment, using public funds to prime the private pump. Relatively small investments by the government can stimulate massive private investment, creating hundreds of thousands of new jobs.

For instance Industrial Development Bonds in the United States offer tax relief to the private lender on the interest paid on loans for construction and other industrial investment projects. This incentive also serves to lower the rate of return the project has to yield and thus encourages risk-taking.

In the State of New Jersey alone 7 billion dollars of new private investment has been stimulated in this way, creating around 100,000 new jobs. A recent study in Massachusetts found that annual growth in new jobs in companies using IDBs was over 24%. More jobs.

This is the sort of gearing of public and private money we need. Government grants to regional and local enterprise agencies. More jobs.

Last year the government turned down nearly 100 million pounds in Derelict Land Grants. Yet every pound of grant produces £6 of new private investment. We will use those grants to the full. More jobs.

Home Improvement and Repair Grants should be expanded yet the government is cutting them back — a curious decision in all conscience when new housing starts are at such a low level, and half a million homes in Britain lack sanitation. Even more indefensible when you reflect that each pound of home improvement grant can generate up to £30 of private investment. More Home Improvement Grants, more jobs.

Government could help our exporters, too, by an effective partnership, where soft loans and guarantee finance were readily available for large overseas orders. What about the government paying for feasibility studies, as the USA did in Hong Kong before winning the order to build the new airport, with lucrative orders for a consortium of American companies? Here of all places Britain should have been on the inside track. More help to exporters, more jobs.

This partnership approach between government and the private sector is the way to generate investment. It is the Alliance approach. More financial partnership, more jobs.

The Alliance government will roll up its sleeves positively to help regenerate the economy, rather than stand back and wring its hands like this government.

The Alliance government will work with industry instead of threatening them with direction and penalties as Mr Hattersley would like to do. In short, the Alliance government will be an enabling government, not, like Labour would be, a disabling government. That is what I mean by becoming partners in one nation.

The Alliance is not static and it cannot be so. We are moving closer, working together better, sparking off ideas on each other.

We have substantial joint policy efforts which are now feeding into the deliberative processes of the two parties. Joint economic and constitutional proposals; a thoughtful and well-considered document from the joint commission on Northern Ireland; and next year we expect to have the Report of the joint commission on Defence and Disarmament before us.

Do not imagine, as you sometimes read in the press, that the purpose of these Commissions is to find the lowest common denominator of agreement between two inflexibly opposed positions. Their purpose is not to negotiate but to reason together. It is to deploy new thinking and new expertise with the help of distinguished Commission memberships from inside and outside the parties. We need that stream of new ideas and we should welcome it. It will strengthen the Alliance.

And don't undersell one of the greatest virtues of the joint leadership of our Alliance. A Prime Minister with a deputy PM who is leader of his own party will bring to an end the quasi-Presidential system of government where one person's views, prejudices and constant meddling interfere with the judgement and collective responsibility of a strong cabinet team.

When we win power you will have to go back to 1906 to find a parallel occasion when the cabinet consisted of so many people who had not held office before. Yet what was the verdict on that government?: "There has not been throughout British history a more talented team of men in government" — wrote one historian adding: "four became Prime Ministers" — that should be enough to keep everybody happy.

There should be no confusion about the Alliance aim: we want to take power, to share power, and to use power:
– to take power away from those who have misused it for so long and put it back in the hands of the majority of the British people;
– to share power in every community, throughout the nation and with those in Parliament who seek the common good;
– to use power to help the helpless and to give new hope to the hopeless, both within and beyond these shores.

That is our aim.

The recovery of the country now rests with our Alliance.

When the French revolutionaries raised the battle cry of 'liberty, equality and fraternity', they stirred the whole of Europe.

Since then millions of words have been spoken and written on liberty. It is a central concern of ours.

Volumes have been produced on equality. It too is a concern of ours.

But what has happened to fraternity? That is what has been trampled underfoot in Britain for so many years. That is what we alone can recapture.

John Stuart Mill — in what might have been a premonition of Thatcherism and Socialism alike — wrote:

"A state which dwarfs its men in order that they may be more docile instruments in its hands will find that with small men no great thing can really be accomplished."

Our task is to enable every individual to flourish, to grow tall, to join us in achieving great things. *We will have to redouble our efforts.* I say to those who've been watching over these last two weeks at home — don't just sit on the sidelines and cheer us on. Come in and join us now because

> *There is a tide in the affairs of men*
> *Which, taken at the flood, leads on to fortune;*

On such a full sea are we now afloat.

The tide has been out — for Liberalism and for Britain — for too long. Our nation has been beached, strewn with the rocks of class conflict, our economy left high and dry by our competitors, our institutions stagnant and our people stranded. But now we can all sense the change and take heart. Our message to Britain is:

Here comes the turn

Here comes the turn of the tide.

Conclusion

Member of Parliament for over twenty years and Liberal Leader for ten, David Steel, more than most, appreciates how long it takes for new ideas to take root and how resistant British political institutions are to change. If, as Harold Wilson once claimed, a week is a long time in politics, the last decade for David Steel must sometimes have seemed an eternity.

Some would wish to believe that all was much as before — after all, despite 26 Alliance MPs, the green leather benches of the House of Commons are filled overwhelmingly with the comfortable products of a seemingly unassailable two-party system. Radical realignment; the search for a new majority, the spirit of co-operation and consensus — whatever the descriptive phrase, the search for the Holy Grail seems as far distant as ever in 1986, in the inhospitable climate of Thatcher's Britain. Buttressed by a massive Tory Parliamentary majority, the citadel remains secure.

And yet much is altered — irreversibly and irrevocably — through the hand of David Steel.

That is undoubtedly true of the Liberal Party. Even if it wished, it cannot retrace its steps back into the garden of lost content where, shut out of British politics, it would again be free to bask in the sunshine of irrelevance, its ideas and policies unsullied by contact with power.

After all, it is no longer alone. Having acted as midwife at the birth of the SDP — and having resisted Cyril Smith's advice to commit political infanticide, by strangling the new Party at the outset — the Liberals have to live with the consequences.

Merger is in any case long overdue. Public disagreements between the two wings of the Alliance over policy, like that on nuclear weapons, have been no greater than those within the Conservative Cabinet — on Westlands, public spending or British Leyland — or within the Labour Opposition's Shadow Cabinet — over defence or nuclear power, for example. And yet there is a difference, for, unlike its rivals, the Alliance possesses no ostensibly democratic means of reconciling what are perfectly natural differing viewpoints and arriving at a common approach. Instead, they must rely on an unsatisfactory and rather seedy process of bargaining, involving the two leaders.

This is one area of special vulnerability, but the notion of "two distinct parties, working in a close Alliance" presents others. It is the Achilles' heel of the Alliance which Tory and Labour will probe mercilessly. The Alliance would do better to listen to its supporters, and those tempted to give it their support, who are impatient with, and confused by, the two Parties' insistence on protecting their separate labels, practices and structures. The voters' concern is solely in backing a unified and effective challenge to the ethos of class-based politics.

So, for the Liberals, there can be no retreat. If the Alliance were to end, the SDP would remain, ally no longer. Frankenstein would not easily be persuaded back into the laboratory; and the SDP would be unlikely to accept that it should end its short life the object of "spare-part" surgery, by friend and foe alike.

But the Liberals *have* changed. A recurrent theme of David's leadership has been his impatience with the Party's lack of professionalism, its labyrinthine system of internal committees, its amiable disregard for electoral presentation. The crude caricature of a dishevelled but lovable Party, in corduroy and open-toe sandals and munching nut cutlets, may have stuck once, but has long since been shaken loose by the 'bumpy ride' promised by the Liberal Leader in his first Assembly speech.

The Party organisation has been shaken up, its committee and decision-making structures streamlined and its ability to use its political opportunities immeasurably enhanced. The annual Party Assembly — a major shop window for displaying what the Liberals have to offer to the voters — has moved a long way from amiable

anarchy towards one of rigorous media management. Last year, at the
Dundee Conference, a notable opponent to apartheid, though not a
member of the Party and only an Observer at the Assembly was
nonetheless encouraged to speak in the debate which formed Party
policy on South Africa. Not an eyebrow was raised at this astute move
by the Assembly managers — but ten years ago, such a step would
have been an unthinkable intrusion upon the Party's democratic
process of policy-making.

Of course, the charge is still made, recently by a Tory MP in the
columns of the *Daily Telegraph*, that the Liberal Party is the "bran and
brown bread brigade". No longer a particularly telling insult in any
case, this attempt to caricature the Liberal Party simply does not
correspond to the reality directly experienced by many millions of
British citizens. The Alliance now runs 24 local authorities, shares in
the administration of a further 20 and exercises a balancing influence
in more than fifty others. Altogether, over one hundred local
authorities — one-in-five of all in Britain — are under Alliance power
or influence, with budgets running into many millions of pounds.
Even if those three thousand Councillors were known universally to
have a penchant for breakfast laxatives — or for Volvos and claret for
that matter — it does not appear to have weighed heavily with the
electorate.

Ironically, the very body which once was characterised as being
most critical of David Steel's strategy — the Association of Liberal
Councillors — has become the leading proponent of "coalition
politics" — on a local level, at least — and a major force for
encouraging a more professional approach to organisation, to
publications and publicity and to political campaigning.

In 1976, in his first Assembly speech, David Steel uttered the words
which he was advised to stifle: that the Party might probably have to
share power with somebody else, at least temporarily, to bring about
change.

That statement in 1986 appears unexceptional — a truism, and
utterly bland in its obviousness. It underscores the everyday
experience of a thousand Alliance Councillors. But the passage of
those ten years in between marked the traumatic movement of the
Liberal Party from the political nursery to maturity. The "coalition
argument"; the Lib/Lab Pact; the Alliance; the balance of power — all
these were measured steps on the path David Steel had chosen to
tread.

The second qualitative change has been in electoral support.

In the 1950s, the golden age of two-Party politics, the Labour and Conservative Parties shared more than 90% of the vote between them. Little movement occurred from Left to Right; swings were uniform and measurable; the object of interest was the small band of 'floating voters' whose fickle behaviour determined the outcome of general elections.

All that has changed. The proportion of votes devoted to the two principal Parliamentary Parties has declined steadily at successive elections. Little over a third of the electorate can be counted upon to support the Conservatives in the worst of all times — and rather less for Labour (as the last election demonstrated).

Yet at present, it is virtually inconceivable that the Conservative vote will fall below 34%, which in itself will be a drop of 8.4% on the 1983 election, and one of its lowest totals in modern history.

Equally, it is difficult to imagine that the Alliance, with 25% of the vote in 1983 and consistently registering nearer 30% in the opinion polls in 1986, would not be able to poll around that figure in the forthcoming general election.

On present indications, Labour might expect to improve considerably on its abject performance in 1983 — although the climb from 27% to near 40%, and an overall majority, is a formidable one.

The state of local politics across Britain suggests the emergence of a genuine three-party system. At a national level, the 1987/88 General Election promises to be the most open since 1923, with each of the three parties beginning the campaign with the support of around one-third of the electorate.

More precisely, the psephological evidence of the last few years, and of 1986 — of Labour's triumph at Fulham, and the Alliance's victory at Ryedale (and, so nearly, at West Derbyshire) — indicates the replication of the two-party system in different guises: in places, a Labour-Tory struggle; elsewhere, Alliance-Tory; sometimes Labour-Alliance; and, in Scotland and Wales, a struggle involving a fourth dimension, the Nationalists.

Whatever the results will be in terms of seats, voting patterns have been fundamentally altered in the last decade.

The third change has been in the realm of ideas. Disraeli warned that: "England does not love coalitions", but the experience of the Lib/Lab Pact, of the formation of the Alliance, and of local government over much of Britain has prepared the electorate for the possibility of multi-party government after the next election. Class-based politics is on the wane, and 'conviction' politics is losing its appeal. The people of Britain are now receptive to the notion of creating a new national consensus and of revamping the political system so that it permits a far greater degree of local autonomy and no longer acts as a powerful break on economic regeneration.

The age of large-scale production, of central direction and corporate control is giving way to small-scale enterprise, to decentralised economic activity and to greater personal responsibility over the production of wealth (through wider share ownership, profit sharing and increasing control at the work place).

That has not been accompanied by a desire to repudiate public services — and Mrs. Thatcher's assault on the National Health Service, on Education, on the Social Services and on Local Government has aroused great hostility.

A sense of social responsibility remains — albeit with an impatience at the ponderous bureaucracy of much of the public sector.

The time is therefore ripe for this greater individual freedom in economic affairs to be matched by new political structures, allowing diversity, flexibility and greater local control. That much has been a consistent preoccupation of David Steel's thinking and looks increasingly to be "an idea whose time has come".

The fourth change is in David Steel himself. Time and time again, his opponents (and sometimes his colleagues) have underestimated his capabilities and his shrewd political strength. The 'Boy David', despite his apparent fresh innocence, is no pushover, as many have found to their cost.

Opinion polls have consistently recorded that he is Britain's most popular political leader. His electoral appeal is widespread and few can match his mastery of television where his performances can be devastatingly effective.

A leader in the new mould, the contrast with Mrs. Thatcher could not be more striking. He eschews the abrasive and domineering approach of the 'conviction' politician, but he also rejects the compromise and drift which has so characterised the leadership of the Labour Party in the last two decades.

The experience of the last ten years has revealed his ability to confront the difficult decisions — despite those who have invariably counselled a more prudent and evasive course.

The next election will be a critical one — for the cause of realignment, for the Alliance and the Liberals, and for David Steel himself. An overall majority for Tory or Labour; a sudden second election for which the Alliance might not be prepared; or a big vote, but no real addition to the Alliance Parliamentary strength: any, or all, of these would suggest a dogged resilience to change which might prove too much even for the persistence and vision of David Steel.

On the other hand, if the outcome of the election is the long-awaited breakthrough into Government, in whatever shape or form, then David Steel's decade of realignment could well be followed by his decade of power. If so, it is a future which he has created — and one which surely he deserves.